Secret no more!

Edited by Jonathan Løw

Secret no more!

45 successful business people share their secrets about
innovation, entrepreneurship and leadership

CONTENTPUBLISHING

Secret no more!
45 successful business people share their secrets about innovation, entrepreneurship and leadership
Edited by Jonathan Løw

© 2018 Jonathan Løw and Content Publishing A/S

First published in Denmark by Content Publishing A/S

Publishing editor: Birgitte Lie Suhr-Jessen
Cover design and layout: www.wehoo.dk

First edition 2018
ISBN 978-87-93607-29-3

Print: BoD GmbH / Ingram Lightning Source
Printed in Germany / Worldwide 2018

Content Publishing A/S
Frederiksdalsvej 228, DK-2830 Virum
www.contentpub.eu

contentpub.eu

CONTENTPUBLISHING

CONTENTS

CONTENTS

Innovation 2

CONTENTS

Leadership

3

INTRODUCTION

Secret no more! is a collection of articles written by 45 successful entrepreneurs, leaders and innovators from across the globe.

I've come to know these inspiring people through 18 years of working with entrepreneurship, innovation and leadership. Some of them are my good personal friends, and others I've only talked to on Skype or emailed loads of times back and forth with.

Secret no more! contains insights from both young tech gurus, experienced top-level CEOs, leadership experts and social entrepreneurs.

All 45 contributors generously share their ideas and best practice, when it comes to creating and scaling a startup, innovating within existing companies and leading with authenticity and passion.

Most of the articles and interviews in the book are new, and some have been published before on personal blogs on the internet.

I hope that when you read this book, you will feel even more inspired to pursue your dreams and goals in life. To put your dent in the universe.

Jonathan Løw
editor of Secret no more!

ENTREPRENEURSHIP

MOGENS THOMSEN
To a more entrepreneurial world

Mogens Thomsen is a Scandinavian entrepreneur specialist. He is the owner of Thomsen Business Information that publishes business information on the web (www.dynamicbusinessplan.com) and apps

I love to promote the entrepreneurial mentality, as I believe it releases energy and sets one free to create value for oneself and one's society. I have chosen to publish free business plan information in plain language as my contribution to a more entrepreneurial world.

You already possess the personal resources

The German philosopher Goethe once said that as soon as you can truly say "Yes I will do it," the necessary personal resources will surface from the inner you and all your life competencies, experience and people around you will be at your disposal. If you can truly say "I want to start a business," you will experience that a lot of resources suddenly will be at your disposal. As soon as you believe in your idea, all you need is the structure to describe your business idea.

10 steps to startup

The 10 steps I will present cover all the major business aspects you need to make decisions about. If you understand the content of these aspects, you know how to navigate in the business environment. The steps are:

1. Business Concept

A good idea is only a good business idea if you are able to make enough money from selling it, for you to live the life you choose. It takes time to formulate a good business idea.

2. Personal Resources

Starting a small business is a very personal thing, because typically you will be the only person present in the company at start. The company therefore must be built on your competencies or the team you put together – and the resources Goethe mentioned.

3. Your product or service

The product or service you offer is the lifeblood of your business. Thus, it is important to analyze its various aspects and to be sure customers like it.

Can you describe your product in one sentence, and what value it gives your customers?

4. Market Description
Before you will be able to carry out any sort of sales or marketing action, you need to identify the market you want to penetrate. Who will most likely be your customers?

5. Sales and Marketing
Sales and marketing are your tools used to approach potential customers. You have to choose the best marketing tools for your specific business. Is it digital marketing, or a signpost in front of your door?

6. Practical Organizing
You need to describe the every-day running of your company, e.g. which business form to choose, how to make accounts, which insurances to take out?

7. Development of the business
Which plans do you have for your business? Grow bigger, or make sure you have time together with your family?

8. Your budgets
Budgets are the above topics described in economic terms. The more specific your business plan is, the easier it becomes to create budgets. Budgets are not so difficult to make. Just make one budget line at a time. E.g.: 2 office chairs at 50 $ = 100 $, then on to next budget line.

9. Financing the Startup
Financing merely means: "How do I raise the funds I need to start my own business?" Where will you get your funds? Yourself, family, banks, suppliers, friends, investors …

10. Dynamic Business
Describing a new business is not a linear task. When you in a business plan write about aspect 9 Financing, the former aspects might already be obsolete. Your new business must be dynamic, but you do not have to re-write the business plan every day. Write the business plan one time and then learn to act cleverly on the changes that are constantly re-shaping the different inter-connected aspects in the business plan.

CHRIS GUILLEBEAU
Checklist for entrepreneurs

Chris Guillebeau is the New York Times best selling author of The Happiness of Pursuit, The $100 Startup, and other books. During a lifetime of self-employment, he visited every country in the world (193 in total) before his 35th birthday. Every summer in Portland, Oregon he hosts the World Domination Summit, a gathering of creative, remarkable people.

1. Ensure that your product or service has a clear value proposition. This is super important! USP means "unique selling proposition" and refers to the one thing that distinguishes your offering from all others. Why should people pay attention to what you are selling? You must answer this question well.

2. Decide on bonuses, incentives, or rewards for early buyers. How will they be rewarded for taking action?

3. Have you made the launch fun somehow? (Remember to think about non-buyers as well as buyers. If people don't want to buy, will they still enjoy hearing or reading about the launch?)

4. If your launch is online, have you recorded a video or audio message to complement the written copy?

5. Have you built anticipation into the launch? Are prospects excited?

6. Have you built urgency – not the false kind but a real reason for timeliness – into the launch?

7. Publish the time and date of the launch in advance (if it's online, some people will be camped out on the site an hour before, hitting the refresh button every few minutes).

8. Proofread all sales materials multiple times . . . and get someone else to review them as well.

9. Check all web links in your shopping cart or payment processor, and then double-check them from a different computer with a different browser.

Next steps

10. If this is an online product, is it properly set up in your shopping cart or with PayPal?

11. Test every step of the order process repeatedly. Whenever you change any variable (price, order components, text, etc.), test it again.

12. Have you registered all the domains associated with your product? (Domains are cheap; you might as well get the .com, .net, .org, and any very similar name if available.)

13. Are all files uploaded and in the right place?

14. Review the order page carefully for errors or easy-to-make improvements. Print it out and share it with several friends for review, including a couple of people who don't know anything about your business.

15. Read important communications (launch message, order page, sales page) out loud. You'll probably notice a mistake or a poorly phrased sentence you missed while reading it in your head.

16. Have you or your designer created any custom graphics for the offer, including any needed ads for affiliates or partners?

17. Set a clear monetary goal for the launch. How many sales do you want to see, and how much net income? (In other words, what will success look like?)

18. Advise the merchant account or bank of incoming funds.

19. Create a backup plan for incoming funds if necessary (get an additional merchant account, plan to switch all payments to PayPal, etc.).

20. Can you add another payment option for anyone who has trouble placing an order?

21. For a high-priced product, can you offer a payment plan? (Note: It's common to offer a slight discount for customers paying in full. This serves as an incentive for customers who prefer to pay all at once while providing an alternative for those who need to pay over time.)

The night before

22. Clear as much email as possible in addition to any other online tasks so you can focus on the big day tomorrow.

23. Write a strong launch message to your lists of readers, customers, and/or affiliates.

24. Prepare a blog post and any needed social media posts (if applicable).

25. Set two alarm clocks to ensure that you're wide awake and available at least one hour before the scheduled launch.

The big morning

26. Schedule your launch time to suit your audience, not you.

27. Soft launch at least ten minutes early to make sure everything is working. It's better for you to find the problems than to have your customers find them!

28. Write the first three to five buyers to say thanks and ask, "Did everything go OK in the order process?" (Side benefit: These buyers are probably your biggest fans anyway, so they'll appreciate the personal check-in.)

29. As long as it's possible, send a quick personal note to every buyer in addition to the automated thank-you that goes out. (If it's not possible every time, do it as often as you can.)

30. Most important: Ask for help spreading the word. Many readers, prospects and acquaintances will help by telling their friends and followers, but you have to ask them.

31. Write to affiliates with a reminder about the new offering.

32. Write to journalists or media contacts, if appropriate.

33. Post on Twitter, Facebook, LinkedIn and any other social networks you already participate in. (It's not usually a good idea to join a new network just to promote something.)

34. Write the general thank-you message that all buyers will receive when purchasing.

35. If applicable, write the first message for your email follow-up series that buyers will receive.

36. Outline additional content for future communication and plan to schedule it after you recover from the launch.

Going above and beyond

37. How can you overdeliver and surprise your customers with this product? Can you include additional deliverables or some kind of unadvertised benefit?

38. Is there anything special you can do to thank your customers? (For a high-price launch, send postcards to each buyer; for something extra, call a few of your customers on the phone.)

The second to last step

39. Don't forget to celebrate. It's a big day that you've worked up to for a long time. Go out to your favorite restaurant, have a glass of wine, buy something you've had your eye on for a while, or otherwise do something as a personal reward. You've earned it.

The very last step

40. Start thinking about the next launch. What can you build on from this one? What did you learn that can help you create something even better next time? Remember, many customers will support you for life as long as you keep providing them with great value. It's much easier to sell to an existing customer than to a new one, so work hard to overdeliver and plan ahead for the next project.

DAN NORRIS
My first business idea

Dan Norris is an award-winning content marketer and the author of the best selling business book The 7 Day Startup.

In June 2013 after failing at entrepreneurship for 7 years, he founded wpcurve.com, a worldwide team of WordPress developers, providing unlimited small fixes and support, 24 / 7 for $69 per month. It became profitable in 23 days, and 14 months later has 21 staff, 500 customers and continues to grow at 15-20% per month.

Dan is a passionate content marketer and has created 600+ pieces of content around entrepreneurship, WordPress and online marketing. In 2013 he was voted Australia's best small business blogger by the readers of Telstra's Smarter Business Ideas magazine.

In 2014 Dan released The 7 Day Startup, which became a top 10 best seller in 3 Amazon categories.

I was two weeks away from giving up on entrepreneurship for good. I flicked through the limited job opportunities in my area and considered moving my family back to the city.

I'd thought of myself as an entrepreneur for the last 14 years. I'd ridden the rollercoaster of business ownership for the last seven. 'What the fuck was the point?', I thought to myself.

My first business idea

I got my first taste of entrepreneurship 14 years ago.

It was the year 2000 and I was a long-haired 20-year-old, struggling through university. I was also bored out of my brain and needed to choose an elective to make up for the courses I had failed. I stumbled across a brand new subject called 'Entrepreneurship'.

I dreamed of launching and running my own successful startup, so this course grabbed my attention.

The goal of the course was to come up with a business idea and plan how to make it happen. I was doing a business degree, so I figured it made sense to choose at least one course that taught me about starting and running a business.

In 2000, it was Dogpile and Hotbot that I used to search the web. But there wasn't much there. All of the good stuff was in the library.

I was majoring in Human Resources and in the library one day, I stumbled across a publication called the Ultimate HR Manual. I hid it so no one else could find it. It couldn't leave the building – it was too powerful.

The manual held all of the secrets for managing human resources. It outlined exactly how to hire and fire, how to recruit amazing talent, how to manage change, how to build a team and how to train. It was the holy grail of HR.

I needed a business idea and after I discovered the HR manual, it dawned on me.

"What if I put the HR manual ... online! I could create a site where business owners could access all of the forms and processes required for best practice HR, including position descriptions, employee surveys, HR audits and training programs. That would be cool! Wouldn't it?"

My first business idea was born.

I spent 6 months planning out the idea, working out exactly what topics to include, how to deliver the documents, how to charge and even how to employ writers.

This was my million dollar idea. HR managers were already paying thousands of dollars for HR staff, so I figured they would certainly pay a few hundred dollars for every document they could ever need. As far as my research revealed, nothing like this existed.

I was proud of my plan – it was very organized, meticulous and thorough. I nervously submitted it with hopes of earning a great mark.

I waited ... and waited for my results. Finally, the day came. I opened the assignment and saw an A – BOOM!

There was one problem.

I didn't launch the business.

Sure, I had created a beautiful business plan after spending countless hours in the library deep diving into painstaking research.

But launching a business wasn't in the marking criteria.

Looking back, the timing was perfect. I had this idea just after the first dot-com crash and services like this became mainstream a few years later. HR documents and policies were easy to share and buy online. In hindsight – I'm sure it had the potential to be a seven or eight figure business.

I will never know for sure.

I learned a very valuable lesson from my failure to launch.

You can never predict what happens after you start a business. Long-term plans and detailed documents are pointless. Most businesses go on to do something very different to what they set out to do. Today, this is called a pivot.

The lesson is "You don't learn until you launch".

My first business
The reason I use the term 'startup' is because I think the term 'business' is very misunderstood.

A startup needs to be high-growth and is usually in a big market with big potential. A startup needs to have the potential of becoming a 'real business', not just a job for its founder.

I've found that the term 'business' often means working for yourself.

Skip forward to 2006 – I had just earned a promotion at my cushy corporate role, I was 26 and I was finally ready to start a business. I told everyone that I would be a millionaire before I was 30.

I had another idea. I would start a business building websites for people. The fact that I didn't know how to build a website and had no IT qualifications didn't bother me.

Instead, I threw myself in at the deep end. I learned rapidly from reading books and by doing the work. My new clients would ask me questions like:

'Can you build a website using ASP?'

I would say yes, then frantically search Google for ASP to find out what it was and get to work.

Everything looked great early on. I landed a project in my first week and earned $40,000 in my first year. Sure, it wasn't exactly $1,000,000 – but I was happy to have even lasted a whole year!

In year two, I generated around $80,000 in revenue and in Year 3 I had eclipsed the hallowed six figure mark.

Before I knew it, I had an office, local employees, a server, a phone system, hundreds of clients and an influx of new leads.

I had built a real business. I was on the path to becoming a millionaire. Or so I thought.

However, I had one major problem.

The business was not profitable. It wasn't profitable in year one, year seven or anywhere in between.

I didn't become a millionaire before 30. I went backwards as all of my friends went forward. I was 30, living week to week, renting and earning a lower wage than anyone I knew.

It got worse before it got better.

I realized that bringing in more revenue wouldn't solve my profitability problem. My business was not growing. I tried everything, and I mean everything, to make it work.

No matter what I did, I couldn't move the needle.

I'd have big successes like winning a $20,000 project, then a big failure like writing off a $10,000 invoice or hiring the wrong person. It was never consistent.

I regularly worked at Christmas time to appease my worst clients.

I struggled with loneliness, a lack of motivation and confidence. I had put myself out there, leaving my friends and co-workers. I knew people expected big things. I expected big things. But I never expected to fail.

I had plenty of positive signs where I'd think things were coming good, but then something would change and I'd be knocked back on my arse again. This happened all. the. time.

I lost faith in my own judgement. I committed to various courses of action, thinking they would save my business, only to have each one fail.

After seven years in business I was turning over about $180,000 per year, but was still only making around $40,000 per year.

In the end, I accepted that it was a problem I couldn't solve. I sold the business to try to build something new.

This time, I was going all in. I wanted to build something real. A startup that would succeed spectacularly. I wanted to stop scraping by and finally become a success.

Not only that, I wasn't leaving any room for the alternative.

I had enough money from the sale to cover 12 months of expenses. If I couldn't get traction by then, I would have to move cities and get a job. This was scary, but it didn't seem like a real threat because I was confident that I could make it work.

My first startup

I knew what to do this time. I was going to create something big, something that could scale. I had four possible ideas I could run with.

A pot plant stand that supported heavy pots – a friend had told me they couldn't find one.

A surfing app that allowed surfers to check into their local break – think Foursquare for surfers.

An SEO app that enabled website owners to order SEO services for keywords.

An analytics dashboard that simplified analytics from various places.

I worked on all of these ideas and then decided to choose one to focus on.

I had no idea about product design or manufacturing, so the pot plant stand was out. I couldn't foresee making any money from the surfing app, so that was out too. I started building the SEO app and Google introduced new rules that punished that style of link building. Strike 3.

The analytics dashboard was the remaining idea, so I ran with it. I named it Web Control Room and later renamed it to Informly, to make it sound more like a startup.

Some things were the same. Throughout the 12 months, most of the time I felt things were going well. I had good traction on my website, a lot of free signups, regular press coverage and I achieved a lot. I had a great team, I put together a solid application that was unique, useful and solved a big problem according to what people said.

After 11 months and trying everything, I was earning just $476 in recurring monthly revenue and spending $2,000+ a month. I had burned through all of the money I made on the first business and was two weeks away from completely running out.

I started looking at jobs and wondering how we'd go about moving back to the closest city where the jobs were.

I'd failed again.

This time it was looking like there was no coming back.

My 7 day success

I had two weeks left, so I had one last crack.

This would be my last startup attempt.

I learned a lot from my first and second business, so I wanted to try to apply this to my new idea. This time, I didn't have seven years or 11 months. At the end of the week, I needed traction on the idea, or I would have to shut everything down and start job hunting.

I was running mainly on adrenaline. I ignored a lot of the activities I would typically spend time on when planning a business. I was focusing only on things that led me to paying customers.

I forgot about:

Sexy ideas. I wanted to solve a problem, sell a service and fast.

My failure. I had failed a lot in 14 years, but I didn't have time to worry about my shortcomings.

Permission. I used to ask for people's opinions on my ideas, but not this time.

Assumptions. There was no time to plan for events based on assumptions.

The small stuff. I didn't have months to agonize over a logo, business name or design – I chose the idea, invented a name and put the site up in one day.

Pricing strategy. I set a price and would let my customers tell me whether it was worth it.

The perfect payment gateway. Informly's payment gateway took 6 months to set up – this time, I used a PayPal button which I set up in 30 minutes.

On Saturday, I decided to launch WP Live Ninja (now WP Curve). My WordPress support service offered unlimited small WordPress jobs, 24 / 7 for $69 per month.

By Saturday afternoon the domain was registered, on Tuesday the site was live, and by Wednesday I sent out an email launching the service. I landed my first paying customer that day.

In the first week, I signed up 10 customers. This resulted in $476 of recurring monthly revenue, which was the exact amount I'd worked up to during the previous 12 months with Informly.

This may not sound like much, but my excitement was through the roof! I knew this was the one. People were voting with their wallets. WordPress issues are an annoying problem that people are prepared to pay for. It was a monthly recurring service in a big market that I knew could scale into something significant.

Within 23 days I was covering costs, and within a month my San Francisco-based co-founder, Alex, had joined me. The thoughts of moving to get a job were a distant memory.

Each month we grew by around 15%. People started proactively spreading the word. After 10 months we had signed up 230 customers and were making over $15,000 monthly recurring revenue (MRR).

After 10 months WP Curve had more customers than my original agency, more annual revenue, more staff and a stronger team, lower costs, a simpler business model, happier customers and three times more profit.

Most importantly, it was a real business. A high-growth startup, in a big market with a lot of potential.

After 14 years, I'd finally realized my dream of being an entrepreneur running a high-growth startup.

It only took seven days.

CHRISTINA HEMBO
Entrepreneurship is first and foremost hard work

Christina Hembo is a Danish designer, entrepreneur and owner of Christina Jewelry & Watches.

- Getting good ideas

- Trying out good ideas

- Creating a hole in an existing market

Being an entrepreneur is not about re-inventing the wheel, nor nerding in a workshop for years like Gyro Gearloose, and suddenly wow! the brilliant idea is there. Entrepreneurship is hard and methodical work that always demands a basic idea, but which can easily build on something that already exists – a product or a market.

For me, being an entrepreneur is synonymous with developing things, getting inspiration, being creative, building on something, and in the process finding the original idea that can be turned into something genuinely new and different.

When I studied design at the University of the Arts in London at the beginning of the new millennium, I was, apart from my professional development, open to inspiration coming from the outside. I took it on board, adapted it, let myself be influenced by my surroundings. The shapes and forms in the city, cars and buildings, people and clothes. Or I left the city and absorbed things there. Back home to Denmark, perhaps right down to the marshes and the area around Tønder, where my design training had its start.

Then comes the connection, the point when education turns into work. For me, the connection was a concrete business idea that combined both of them. My then boyfriend, now husband, Claus, and I had spotted a hole in the watch market. Not a gigantic hole, but one that we could expand. And that rhymed with one of my entrepreneurship points: Creating a hole in an existing market.

Claus and I flew quite a bit between London and Denmark, predominantly with the discount airline Ryanair. Flying was still a luxury 10-15 years ago, but the concept – make the product accessible for many people and focus on the volume rather than a high profit – would also become the starting point for our idea.

I designed a quality watch with real diamonds. We priced it according to a market that we believed more people should have access to. Swiss-made as a mark of quality for the watch – diamond as an expression of authenticity and luxury. With the mantra "affordable luxury" as the common thread for our watch business. I loved watches, Claus had previously sold watches – the perfect match.

We had our stock of watches under my parents-in-law's guest bed. Our first company car was a cheap rental car from the Danish version of Rent-A-Wreck, and our invoices were handwritten. We'd walked from one watchmaker's shop to the next in London and sold our watches. We used the same recipe in Denmark. When we visited trade fairs we travelled at the lowest budget prices, the cheapest hotel – or we slept on the roof of our van. But we got a grip on the market.

I glimpsed a real opportunity to develop my education and personal interest in design into an independent career, also jointly with my husband and partner in life. To succeed at that is, for me, the quintessence of entrepreneurship. The ability to be independent, self-employed and fully integrated professionally with the business dream pursued.

All beginnings are difficult. Or, as I like to repeat: You must work hard to be able to live from your own ideas. Christina Design London, which we were called initially, fought its way in a traditional and conservative market – but a market that both Claus and I had sound backgrounds for doing well in if we didn't compromise on our maxim: Affordable luxury.

My designs had the impact I and the company had hoped for. The idea of always having real diamonds in the watches, the streamlined design, quality production and reasonable prices was a sustainable concept on both the Danish and the international markets – not manifesting itself as an explosion in sales, but in the necessary progress that is often proportional with the work involved. We had discovered and exploited a hole in the existing market. As mentioned, it wasn't large, but it was there, and thereafter it was a task for Christina Design London to widen that hole.

The entrepreneur's faithful companion in my eyes is innovation. There's no sense in having a good idea if you're not constantly in a position to develop it. Innovation is both a natural and an innate part of the entrepreneur's platform. From the very beginning. From the time we entered the watch market in 2004, the ability to innovate has been a conscious driving force. No resting on the laurels along the way.

When the financial crisis hit with great intensity in 2008, we moved from an entrepreneur-based business to an innovation-based business, with the cliché that attack is the best form of defence. We had to take the offensive. Building your own jewelry from separate pieces, from the jewelry branch, which I and we were naturally updated on, was the obvious step to take. Christina Collect was our patented response for the future. So you still bought a Swiss-made watch, and always with a least one diamond, but based on the concept of collecting pieces and building on it – with diamonds as the central focus.

To compare with what Pandora had done for the jewelry branch, the Collect Watch at DKK 995 was in reality our bracelet for generating extra sales. The watch had a bezel that could be screwed off and changed to a more expensive version with more gems, and under the bezel was a flange where additional gems such as sapphire, amethyst or topaz could be mounted. The strap in real Italian leather was easy to change to new colours that matched the gems in and under the bezel. Gems and straps cost from DKK 199, so we held on to the "affordable luxury" principle while enabling the individual customer to continue building up to a quite considerable value.

Christina Collect not only secured a foothold on the market as an innovation, it was also proof for me and us that entrepreneurship cannot stand alone. You must do more. Development or innovation is always the natural consequence of a good idea. That in this case it was also a necessary offensive in a financial crisis on the world market served as the experience we needed to intensify our presence not just in the watch industry but in the jewelry branch as a whole.

Just a few years later, in 2011, we again made a virtue out of necessity. With elbow-grease, idea development and a definitive venture we carried out a paradigm change that was aimed at defining our current company name, Christina Jewelry & Watches, as a distinct jewelry brand. We turned the watch into jewelry – fusing as it were time and jewelry into one thing. For the already unique strap lock we developed a so-called T-bar, which is also a patent today. It's a device that makes it possible to change the watch strap in just a few seconds and pull through leather cords. With tip-top quality again, the cords were produced in real calf- or lambskin and in many colours.

At the same time I could wallow in something close to a dream world of design, down to the minutest details, of dozens of real silver and gold charms to set on the cords.

A profound transformation of our business foundation, but the result of constant innovation in line with an entrepreneur's conceptual way of thinking.

A year after we launched our watch, leather cords and charms, I designed rings that can be built upon, and earrings and necklaces, for the expanded collection. It was yet another product line in the breakthrough on the Danish jewelry scene that neither I nor my husband had seen the extent of when we presented Christina Collect as a pure jewelry brand that built on the same principles as our original idea: Affordable luxury.

Now, three years after our comprehensive change, we're living our dream more intensely than ever. We have grown to three times our size then, and Christina Jewelry & Watches is today the leading jewelry brand and the market leader in Denmark. And we are well on the way, out into the big world, with our own subsidiaries on the largest markets, instead of distributors and private-label customers. We will grow organically, just as we have in Denmark. We will not use our abilities, knowledge, designs, patents and production capacity to enrich primarily others. The gains are our own – and that is, after all, also the entrepreneur's privilege.

For the entrepreneur, the good idea is important as a lever. Just as education, talent, professionalism and focused determination are. In my world, no entrepreneur gets beyond the fringe if he or she isn't ready to put the most important factor into the project over a long time: Hard work …

HERLE JARLGAARD HANSEN
From an insecure quiet mousy to power entrepreneur

Herle Jarlgaard Hansen is 30 years old, born in Svendborg and based in Copenhagen (Denmark). In 2011 she founded FindersKeepers, which is a platform for upcoming designers in various categories. The business is primarily known for its curated design markets in Copenhagen, Aarhus and Stockholm, which gather hundreds of designers and creative entrepreneurs. In 2017 more than 35.000 visited seven FindersKeepers markets.

Herle Jarlgaard Hansen won the prestigious IVÆKSTaward as Female Entrepreneur of the Year in 2015 and in 2016 FindersKeepers won the popular AOK-Award in Copenhagen.

As the CEO of FindersKeepers I meet a lot of entrepreneurs. They are surely very different, but there is a thing they all have in common. They all have this unique power component. I see their passion shine through and I see their drive – which isn't always easy to find anywhere else. They believe in themselves, in their ideas and in the people they surround themselves with.

Someone who doesn't fit this description might be afraid of throwing themselves into the exciting and nerve-wrecking adventures of entrepreneurship. If you are insecure or cautious in generel business questions, you might feel that you'll never be able to fill the shoes of a power entrepreneur, who leads and makes others follow. Also I have no doubt that this role feels more natural to some rather than others, however, confidence and drive aren't necessarily aptitudes that you're born with. At least, I wasn't.

Back in school, I don't think my class mates would have imagined I would end up running my own business and winning the award for female entrepreneur of the year in Denmark. I used to be the quiet, insecure girl who followed the others instead of going first. I always used to worry about what others thought of me and if they liked me. I hated parent meetings at school, because I was always told that I should raise my hand more often in class. Whenever I had exams, I often ended up with low grades, as I went into shutdown mode just thinking of the idea of having to perform. I could only be myself when I was in a safe environment amongst my family and my closest friends. Here I could laugh hard, gesticulate wildly and just be me.

Insecurity tripped me up

When I started FindersKeepers, I never would have thought it would become this great entrepreneurial adventure and something which I could make a living of. I did it because, to me, it was the best fun in the world. I started FindersKeepers while studying at the Royal Design Academy, and for a while I was convinced I was going to be a designer. In the beginning I was still very much the quiet girl and my insecurity and drive to do everything perfectly tripped me up several times.

I'll never forget something that happened at my first FindersKeepers market. Back then there was a second-hand part of the market, so therefore I had been going from store to store in Copenhagen to persuade some of the shop assistants to sell their unused, yet cool clothes. Contacting strangers like this was already far outside my comfort zone. I visited a high-end fashion store in Hellerup with my palms sweating. I had dolled myself up in high heels and my best look, I had even borrowed a friend's expensive Balenciaga bag, to impress the shop assistants. Despite being nervous, I put on my big smile and went into the store, where I politely said hello to the shop assistant and explained my idea to her. Her loud response was, in front of the other customers, what on earth I was thinking, and how I would ever think that she would consider participating in my pathetic flee market. She then asked me to get out of her shop.

It wasn't personal

"Shit", I cried, once I had made it home. I felt so stupid and humiliated, and I allowed my own insecurity to take over. What if she was right? After all, she knew a lot about clothes. Should I even persevere? What if it would be a flop? Today I see that the shop assistant's response wasn't about me or Finders-Keepers. Perhaps this is just how she meets the world with her boxing gloves on, or perhaps she had a really bad day. Whatever made her react in that way, she should have been the one ashamed afterwards, not me.

This episode imprinted itself in my brain, mostly because it awoke a stubborn defiance, which has always been latent, just below the quiet and cautious surface. "Hell no", she would not succeed in getting me down. I decided to focus on all the brilliant people I had come across and who believed in the project and wanted to be part of it. I wanted to prove to everyone that Finders-Keepers would turn out to be a great success.

Once the first market had successfully come to an end, I felt like visiting the shop in Hellerup again, and in the best Pretty Woman style show the shop assistant what she had missed out on.

Although the shop assistant experience might seem somewhat insignificant, it marked a turning point for me. This doesn't mean that my insecurity has completely disappeared, or that I haven't sometimes cried under the duvet after meeting resistance. I've often felt insufficient, but every time this happens my skin grows a bit thicker.

Now I lead the way

In the same way people I went to school with might have found it hard to envision me as an entrepreneur, people who know me now, and didn't know me before FindersKeepers, find it hard to imagine that I was once the quiet, insecure mouse at the back of the classroom, letting others lead the conversation. Over the last six years my development has been almost unbelievable. I don't think I would ever have learned so much about myself if it hadn't been for throwing myself into FindersKeepers. I've pushed boundaries and I've done what had to be done despite the insecure girl inside me quaking in her boots from fear. I've learned to listen to myself and to the people who mean something to me. I have met and still meet incredible, inspiring people, from whom I've learned and still learn skills. I've sweated, laughed and celebrated. I've even come to recognise myself in some of the descriptions that are often used to describe entrepreneurs; power, initiative and drive. It makes me feel proud, that now I'm the one leading the way.

Herle's advice to the new or insecure entrepreneur

Keep the negative feedback in perspective.
One of the most important things, which I've learned as an entrepreneur, is not to take criticism personally.

Don't take criticism personally. Of course it still affects me if someone criticises me or what I do. But I've learned that negative feedback, to a high degree, reflects the person who delivers it. If you know that you're doing your best, and meet people with a positive attitude, and they still respond to you with their arms crossed and negativity, then this isn't about you.

Listen to the ones who matters.
Distinguish between the feedback you receive. Everyone will have an opinion about what you do, and there's no reason to lie awake at night because the postman or your uncle Carl just trashed your business plan. Listen to people you admire, and from whom you can learn. This is where you must absorb all the wisdom possible.

Remember you're the expert in your project.

I've always suffered from heavy exam jitters because I was afraid of not being good enough when I had to perform. This fear has affected me whenever I've had to give interviews or give talks and lectures. Here it has helped to remind myself, that I've actually got a PhD in FindersKeepers. Right now there's nobody who knows more about it than me. And the same goes for you when it comes to your project and your passion. You're the leading expert in your own field.

One step at a time.

You have to start somewhere. It's quite banal, but in one's eagerness to do everything right it's easy to forget. Really this goes for everything you throw yourself into in life. Of course, one can have ambitions and dreams, but nothing will ever be perfect from day one. The most important thing is to get started. There's not a single one of all the brilliant and cool people you'll meet in this book who've started where they are today. FindersKeepers is still far from perfect, I work every day to make it better, and in the end the process is just as fantastic as the result.

Have faith that you will grow with the project.

This advice also applies when it comes to your own personal development. If you're too cautious and introverted, you're unlikely to transform into a outspoken power human overnight. However, trust that you will develop, solve and learn from challenges on your way. Take small steps to challenge your boundaries, and every time you step out of your comfort zone you will grow a little.

SUSANNE HESSELLUND
Where there's a will, there's a way

Already as a child, Susanne Hessellund decided that she wanted to become a helicopter pilot. At the age of 25, she passed her helicopter certificate. After attaining the sufficient amount of flight hours, she was employed by Maersk to become the first female helicopter pilot flying the North Sea. Later she was appointed as captain at a big Canadian corporation, CHC. Susanne founded Bel Air in 1994 and later set up Bel Air Aviation with offshore activities together with a strong team. It is a professional and well-run offshore helicopter company with a base in Esbjerg Airport (Denmark, Europe), where she and her team fly personnel and materials to oil and gas installations, windfarms and vessels in the North Sea.

For me, the most important thing to run a successful company is to have competent, flexible and dedicated employees, who are happy to go to work every day and who will give a unique service to our customers. Caring for our employees and their families is one of the core values at Bel Air. It is essential for me to make room for the whole person. Everyone must be able to balance work and family life – that is the only way to make room for excellence.

A professional and dedicated board is another important cornerstone for success. It is important that the board covers all the necessary competencies, so that we can ensure a solid foundation for our helicopter operations, since the start-up demands comprehensive mandatory authorizations, financing of the very expensive offshore helicopters and setting up a team of competent employees with previous experience within aviation.

These were the cornerstones when I started-up Bel Air Aviation – and here is our story behind the start-up of a successful helicopter company:

While working as a helicopter pilot and being part of the establishment of DanCopter, we had kept our little private helicopter company, Bel Air, which was established in 1994 when I passed my helicopter certificate.

In 2007, after leaving DanCopter, we made a big decision: To develop Bel Air for offshore operations. Two years followed with very comprehensive preparations to fulfill the strict demands and requirements to offshore flights. A professional board was established and the right team was set up with competent and experienced employees from the helicopter field.

In 2009, we acquired our first offshore helicopter – we had chosen the Italian manufacturer AgustaWestland. A close relation and great cooperation with AgustaWestland has made it possible to make the dream come true. Agusta-Westland manufacture helicopters for offshore flying, for search and rescue, for the police and similar operations demanding high safety. They have contributed to the configuration of the helicopters so that they are now a perfect match to the Danish North Sea offshore market. AgustaWestland have been part of our journey for many years and they know Bel Air and my family very well – my children have been with me on several trips to Italy to bring home a new helicopter, and our Italian business partners smile, every time I have arrived with a baby in a carry-cot.

I have 6 children, who are from 10 to 24 years old. The children are used to the many hours I spend at Bel Air, on the other hand I really prioritize my free time with them. This goes for the children still living at home as well as for my eldest girls who have flown the nest. Each of my children have their own weekend dedicated to him or her during the year. The time in the evenings is dedicated to my family, but when the last child has been tucked in, I return to my working tasks and this is how I make ends meet. I find the energy in my family, in my colleagues at Bel Air and in myself when alone a few hours every month. When we have set our minds to something, we put all our energy and will into succeeding – this is why Bel Air's motto is: "Where there's a will, there's a way".

The most important asset of Bel Air are our employees, and I always participate when we take on new employees. It is very important for me to ensure that Bel Air's values come naturally to all the new colleagues in our team. We expect from all our employees that they have a positive attitude, that they are flexible, loyal, cooperative and hardworking, and it is also important to have a good sense of humour and, last but not least, at Bel Air we talk with each other – not about each other. Altogether this helps ensure a unique workplace with a fantastic team who can meet the many challenges in a busy workday and still find the positive energy to help each other and have fun together.

Our working hours are flexible so that we may help each other when we have busy periods here at Bel Air. This helps us ensure the high flexibility, which is one of our really strong points. Naturally, this flexibility goes both ways, so you can have extra time for your family between the busy periods. It is important to make room for the whole person, that is the only way we can do our best.

The families behind our Bel Air employees are a natural part of our company, and I am really happy that so many come to our Bel Air parties and family events, or just stop by for a brief visit.

In 2014, we built our new Bel Air Homebase in Esbjerg Airport, and one of the first things added to the plans was a Children's Corner so that the children of our employees can come to work with their mom or dad whenever it suits the plans of the family. The room is designed by my youngest daughter, so it has everything children could wish for, such as a huge TV screen for PlayStation, film and games, a massage chair, comfy bean bag chairs, sofas and lots of games.

We have also done our best to ensure that all employees thrive during their workday in the new building, particularly, our hangar has state-of-the-art equipment and we have thought of all details: Floor heating, daylight, music centre and all the newest tools give our technicians the best possible working conditions to carry out their important work of constantly ensuring maintenance of our helicopters so that safety is always first priority and the helicopters are in perfect condition for the demanding offshore flights.

All in all, it is quite natural that safety, both safety at work and flight safety, have first priority in a company with offshore operations. The passengers who fly by helicopter to their offshore workplace for Maersk, Orsted, Ineos, Hess and Siemens can rest assured that our helicopters and pilots will ensure that they have a safe trip to their workplace in the North Sea and later back home to their families.

Bel Air has been and still is on an exciting voyage. Along the winding road to our goal we have met many challenges, but together the Bel Air team has what it takes – we have come a long way together and I am very proud of our team.

Some good advice to future executives:

- You really need to be enthusiastic about your project – you will probably work around the clock for a very long period of time … if you love what you're doing, it doesn't feel like work … and it will give you a lot of positive energy and challenges.

- Your base and family must be prepared that you have an extra child to care for day and night … your company.

- Appoint a professional board with high expertise to help you ensure all the necessary competencies for your company – legal, financial, contractual, projects, etc.

- Find the right employees with the right attitudes, values and high-level competencies – preferably better than your own, in order to raise the standards and become even better – and most important of all: You must be fond of your employees.

- If your company grows: Set the right management team – Attitudes, values, personal chemistry and competencies must be the right ones so that they can run their departments – preferably better competencies than yourself …

JOE PULIZZI
A wake-up call for me

Joe Pulizzi is the founder of Content Marketing Institute, a UBM company, the leading education and training organization for content marketing, which includes the largest in-person content marketing event in the world, Content Marketing World. Joe is the winner of the 2014 John Caldwell Lifetime Achievement Award from the Content Council. Joe is the author of five books, including his latest, Killing Marketing. His third book, Epic Content Marketing, was named one of "Five Must-Read Business Books of 2013" by Fortune Magazine. You can find Joe on Twitter @JoePulizzi. If you ever see Joe in person, he'll be wearing orange.

Starting a business practice with the content-first mentality is not easy. It will open you up for criticism. To combat this, you'll have to develop thicker skin.

Let me give you a personal example. It's very difficult for me to receive any kind of criticism at all. It affects everything about me. I internalize it, and not always in a positive way. After last year's Content Marketing World, I read all the reviews. Now, while most of the reviews, mind you, were glowingly positive, a few were negative (really negative). Really negative. They didn't like the food. They couldn't get into certain sessions. Some didn't like Cleveland. I was in a bad state about this for days.

In another situation, I received a really negative review on Amazon for my last book, Epic Content Marketing. I just couldn't leave it alone, and I HAD to comment on it. I totally regret that decision, because if you are going against a troll, they will always win.

Why am I telling you this? Because as bad as those things are to me, they help me grow. I understand this now. It's part of what I signed up for. I need to take what I learn from all this feedback and move on. Simply put, we need to move out of our comfort zone sometimes to find growth.

So I had the pleasure of interviewing my friend Ann Handley, Chief Content Officer at MarketingProfs and author of the latest fantastic book, Everybody Writes. Ann had some great information on content marketing, but for this rare episode, I'm going to share this personal story that Ann shared about opting in to life in order to grow. Listen to this episode of Content Inc. to hear Ann's story in her words or read her story below (as told by Ann).

When I was a child I was incredibly shy and extremely introverted. It was so severe that, even within my own family, I was known as the shy one, the quiet one. Part of that is just my role in the family. I am the youngest by far; my siblings are all much older than me – 10, 12, 15 years older than me. So they were always very loud and boisterous. I also grew up in a family where there was a lot of laughter and humor, but I was usually the butt of the joke because I was always doing something stupid, right? [Ann laughs.] So that just made me incredibly introverted and always a little bit anxious about putting myself out there, because I always thought that someone was going to make fun of me.

So I always hung back. People would come to my house and I would literally go hide under the bed until they left; that's how shy and introverted I was. For instance, my parents would have friends over and say, "Don't you want to come out and say hi?" I would be under the bed with a flashlight and book. "No, I'm good," I'd say.

I defined myself as shy and introverted for a long time. By the time I was in fourth grade, I was risk-averse and would say "no" to everything. I was never the kid who did any after-school activities or anything like that.

My fourth-grade teacher was really into having us grow as people and encouraging us to grow as people, not just as scholars. She not only wanted us to learn how to read, write, and so on, but she also wanted us to learn how to speak in front of class and facilitate a discussion. She forced us out of our comfort zones, and I hated it. I had extreme anxiety about going to school, and I got really great at faking sick that year, to the point where my mother was just beside herself thinking that I had some sort of disease. She was convinced I was an incredibly sickly child, but I was just having extreme anxiety about going to see this teacher. You want your kid to have that kind of teacher, but it was terrible.

So it came to a head one day when she sent us to the field hockey field to do some sort of leadership or skill-building exercise with field hockey sticks. If I hated being called out in class, the second thing that I hated was anything to do with gym or athletics or team sports.

She didn't have enough sticks for everyone, so half the kids would go play, and when she blew the whistle they were supposed to swap sticks with those of us on the sidelines.

When she blew the whistle, I got in the line of sight of the jockiest, beefiest girl in my class, and when she came to give me the stick, I said, "You can have a double turn." She was so thrilled, and I thought I was so clever sitting this one out. I never thought the teacher would notice out of 30 kids that I wasn't on the field. She didn't notice that I wasn't on the field, but she did notice that the beefy athletic girl was back on the field, so she asked, "Why are you out here playing again?" She said, "Annie said that she didn't want to so I could go again."

Because my teacher was so into openness, sharing, personal development, and taking responsibility for your mistakes as well as your successes, she made a huge deal about it. She called my mom and dad to have a meeting with the principal.

The worst part about it was that I ended up with a failing grade on my report card for the next semester. That devastated me because I identified as a non-athlete, while I also identified as an incredible student. I was upset if I wasn't the top kid in class. The fact that I got a failing grade was devastating to me because I never identified as a failure and someone who got F's on their report card.

That experience was a wake-up call for me.

Opting out of this means opting out of life, and opting out of opportunities. It would be a while before I would really internalize that lesson, but it definitely started something in me, something where I realized I can't literally sit on the sidelines and expect to succeed.

Ask yourself:

What does this mean for you? What opportunities are you letting go by because they are too difficult? Are you, yourself, your biggest challenge? With so many challenges in front of us, the last thing we need to stop us is the person in the mirror.

THE SECRET OF CHANGE
IS TO FOCUS ALL OF YOUR
ENERGY, NOT ON FIGHTING
THE OLD, BUT ON BUILDING
THE NEW.

Socrates

JØRGEN MADS CLAUSEN
Entrepreneurship, from cradle to grave

Former CEO of Danish company Danfoss Jørgen Mads Clausen is currently the proactive chairman of the company's board. Along with business, he engages with other issues, including debates on social affairs.

For many, the word 'entrepreneurship' denotes the early stage work that goes into startups. In truth, entrepreneurship can be practised at any stage in a company's history. Excitement is there for the entrepreneur in a company that is already doing well. Indeed, there are many advantages to the work in the context of a mature organisation. Examples abound of companies who came close to bankruptcy, yet managed to turn a failing business into a resounding success. Apple is one. Steve Jobs returned to Apple when it seemed the end was nigh; subsequently it became one of the most highly valued companies in the world. There, it was moreover a clear case of a single individual possessed of a certain willpower – Jobs – making the difference. The rescue was not a simple matter.

Likewise, Nokia weathered considerable problems following the collapse of the Soviet Union. Nokia's then product range included televisions, rubber boots and other items whose prospects were far from shiny. Pressed for a solution, the management gave rein to a minor product line in mobile telephony. This brought fame and fortune to Nokia, raising it to the most valuable company in Europe. It was a complete surprise when Nokia, sadly, was overtaken by Apple in the field of mobile phones; the activities were acquired by good old Microsoft, who later sold them on with considerable losses. Microsoft itself had grown through entrepreneurship, creating an operating system for IBM which was to provide the base for the world's first personal computers. After the departure of Bill Gates, a hugely enterprising boss, Microsoft lost that innovative spark. An entrepreneur like Gates wouldn't have cast a glance at Nokia. IBM too, once a highly successful and pioneering computer enterprise, came adrift after its expansion and the departure of the original Watson family: the intrepid spirit was no longer there. Nokia's ground-breaking abilities have perhaps not quite fizzled out, however. They acquired Siemens' stake in the networks joint venture; and rumours say that promising new technology is on the cards.

Such stories of progress and how it was achieved are immensely heartening and instructive to the aspiring entrepreneur. And they need not be about the industry giants we all know. There are plenty of other narratives and biographies that testify to success in business. The role models thus provided are important to our understanding of entrepreneurship, for this is a skill for which the phrase 'learning by doing' might well have been invented. To learn about entrepreneurship at university, a student would have to progress through countless courses such as marketing, business law, finance, accountancy, personnel management, logistics and so forth – to mention only the technical subjects. To develop all the necessary skills in a plethora of disciplines would stretch most of us. Yet some expertise in the area in which you hope to innovate is a necessity. I have at times been astounded at the inadequacy of some of the most successful entrepreneurs in areas where I would have thought their acumen was required. For example, Steve Jobs seems to have been argumentative and difficult to work with; his people skills, if we believe the book about him, were not exactly well developed. Perhaps the success factor in his case was an ability to bring out the very best in those who could tolerate his style. That style might well have been his downfall; it was certainly the reason he was thrown out of Apple in the first place.

What cannot be denied is the fact that entrepreneurship, in all its forms, is a high-risk endeavour! It is all too easy to abandon the whole thing. We hear about the people who succeed; what about those entrepreneurs who didn't make it? There are plenty of such cases. Inconceivably large fortunes, carefully amassed, are lost and never regained. Add to that a plethora of disappointments, cases of lost face, depression, financial ruin, divorce and even suicide. Suffering can affect spouses, children, loyal employees and local communities. The crucial act of preparation for the entrepreneur is that he or she conduct realistic preliminary surveys and devise forecasts that will withstand the criticism of colleagues and mentors and win their backing. Every eventuality must be carefully gone through. In other words, people must be completely sure that a vessel is watertight before it is launched. Every risk should be minimised and others given free rein to criticise your project, even though this act of courage may lead to hurt feelings. The criticism is not personal! Failure is acceptable only when a professional effort has been made – in which case, there is nothing to be ashamed of.

Most entrepreneurs, the world over, fear the shame of failure – the "I told you so" moment. No one wants to take unnecessary risks-yet we do, on a fairly regular basis. Crossing the lights on amber, for instance. This is why your own experience is so important, as well as having an experienced team who can navigate the difficulties that are bound to crop up.

The biggest challenge for almost any entrepreneur is capital and the funding for their idea. In early phases, many projects simply do not get off the ground because their initiators haven't the money and can't convince others to back their idea. In the latter case this might be just as well; a realistic, water-tight business plan is a prerequisite. Many entrepreneurs find, with perhaps a sprinkling of good luck, that their project takes off. They possess the ability to adapt, finding the niche to which their idea is well-suited. This can be the favourable wind that allows them to drive onwards. And this is why it is often far better to practise entrepreneurship in already established companies. The basic organisation is there, with the income and positive cash flow. Perhaps the very thing they need is new ideas and knowledge – which is where the entrepreneur steps in. Now it is a matter of coming to an agreement with the management of this company. Most small and medium-sized firms operate in a scenario like this. Smaller firms will appreciate the addition of good qualifications and specialist expertise; larger companies need someone with in-depth experience and detailed knowledge of the sector. In many cases, buying shares in a company, or even acquiring it, can be a way forward. At this point in time, around 20,000 family businesses in Denmark expect to see a generation change within the next 10 years. You might be the one to grab the baton. Certainly, a wide variety of opportunities exist. If you own a company, there is the option to merge with a company undergoing a generation change. The new generation can stay on as passive shareholders, without the need for acquisition expenses. Further on down the line, you might buy out the family.

In summary, there is a great deal to be said for developing an idea in an existing company, either as a major shareholder or as its owner. Even if you don't own 100 percent of the shares, you will be no worse off than someone who sets out without the necessary capital. In virtually every case, much depends on having to convince others about your plans, but here the risk is significantly less because the company is already up and running. It can also be easier to begin as the company director's right hand man, rather than taking all the responsibility. It seems there are plenty of 'older' companies in which the entrepreneurial spirit has evaporated and where the focus is on avoiding any kind of rough sea. The old products may well endure: they can in fact be the basis for funding the new adventure, which it is your pleasure to provide! Keep the antennae tuned!

IF PLAN A DOESN'T WORK, THE ALPHABET HAS 25 MORE LETTERS.

Claire Cook

TORBEN FRIGAARD RASMUSSEN
Forever entrepreneur

Torben Frigaard Rasmussen served as Special Operating Director at HgCapital. He joined HgCapital in 2014 and works with HgCapital to find new investment opportunities across Scandinavia. He also served as Consultant at Nextedia Société Anonym.

Mr. Rasmussen was the Chief Executive Officer of E-conomic A/S and E-conomic international A/S from 2008 to 2014. He has successfully carried out the merger/integration of Retail Internet within the Come&Stay company.

He has a 20-year track record in the SME software and online sector, working to build businesses in Europe and across the USA. He is an expert in the field of mobile and email marketing. A native speaker in Danish, he is fluent in English and can get by in Swedish and Norwegian as well. Mr. Rasmussen is a graduate from Wharton.

There's an entrepreneur in every successful leader.

Leaders have that restlessness that makes them constantly look for improvements, new options, new markets and more growth. They're eager for change, renewal and development and have respect, but lack an interest in basic operations, reports, long internal meetings and traditional operation assignments.

It is the entrepreneur with the sense of scaling and growth that will become a successful leader.

Sense of scaling is the key phrase, since many talented entrepreneurs don't become leaders of a company with constant growth only because they haven't mastered the scaling. Many entrepreneurs focus on being the 'man of the house' and being part of every aspect of the business; knowing all the customers and employees and to be the center of attention.

This classic entrepreneur will not be able to achieve growth in the long run or on a larger scale. There are many healthy things in being the initiator, the motivator, the center of attention and understanding all aspects of your business, but the change from being a successful entrepreneur to a successful leader is founded on clear principles and a continuous understanding of their own role and function.

Powerful growth isn't the objective for all, but if you want to grow from 10-15 to 100 employees in 1-2 years, not knowing the names of all your employees, having customers you didn't even realize you had, experience the bank beginning to recognize you as a legitimate customer, and suddenly talking about a market value close to a billion, then you can't change paths or principles often.

The bridge between being an entrepreneur and a leader is to keep your entrepreneur mind, but focus on:

Having a joint goal and vision
Have a clear goal set, vision for the company, and being sure that everyone understands and shares it.

Creating a culture and atmosphere of change
Growth means constant changes. Employees, procedures and routines should be constantly revised, so build windmills and don't fence in or exploit change. Motivate and reward reconstruction and renewal. Challenge habits and routines. Experiment, test, take chances and try something new.

Ensuring talented people around you
Growth shapes new needs and no entrepreneur is the best at all positions (even if we often think we are), so employ better people than yourself for specific functions and have confidence in their work.

Hiring carefully, but fire confidently
It's expensive and harmful to get the wrong employee in, so even if there's specific needs, you need to hurry slowly. On the other hand, there isn't time for many chances or hope for change if the employee isn't prepared for the changes that come with growth.

Simplifying the organizational operation
Many non-essential functions can advantageously be outsourced, and a lot of marketing, PR, customer care, knowledge sharing, reporting and information can be automated and done in the cloud rather than in the meeting room.

Accept failures

Change culture is accepting failures. That you test and fail, that you have more faith in the market and customer response than long analyses and reports. It also means that you have to forgive more than you have to grant permissions. Growth-orientated employees and talented management teams must dare to find new and original ways to achieve the common objective.

Celebrate successes

Preserve the joy of small and large successes. Share the good stories and celebrate them!

Maintain open and direct dialogue

Investors, advisors and professional boards are often a prerequisite for growth, but they must not destroy the open and direct dialogue from your entrepreneur days. Provide updates on large screens, share information, give the opportunity for input, criticism and dialogue, and remember change culture rule number 1: The leader must lead the way of change. The leader must continuously change his or her format for involvement with employees, but always with a focus on openness.

Management By Walking Around (MBWA)

Be visible, direct and committed. Have team meetings outside, come uninvited to meetings, have an open office, and meet employees in informal settings. Incidentally, I have never myself had an office in E-conomic (although suddenly it's become trendy for a CEO to not have an office ... just because LEGO did it).

I have personally benefited greatly from continually reminding myself of these essential principles, especially through the hectic times of critical customer initiatives, economic challenges, staffing issues, etc.

It is crucial to create space and room to be both entrepreneur and leader – and it's done best by having clear principles for one's work. A clear goal, a clear vision and a clear message to employees and the outside world can be a fantastic milestone in a hectic time and must be prioritized.

As an example the vision of E-conomic was written in one line:

"We help manage your business by making accounting simpler, social and fun."

This was coupled with our five core values: Transparency, Respect, Ambition, Dedication, Have Fun. This will make a big difference if you as a leader dare to live out your values 100% of the time.

In the same way, it's natural as an entrepreneur not to be interested or engaged in financial numbers, statistics, reports, etc., but it's both a necessary tool for investors and the board of directors, but also to create a feeling of community and belonging, strengthen transparency and to be an inspiration to your employees.

You can't just ignore your "numbers". I love numbers and data. It gives irreplaceable information and you just need to know them ... even more than your banking. But you shouldn't unconditionally be controlled by them. But you should know all relevant KPI's.

Transparency is key. We had monitors all over our offices with all relevant and less relevant information which was updated and accessible 24/7, e.g., number of customers, reactions of blog posts, both positive and negative, the lunch menu, birthdays, guests, new hires, NPS on everything possible, revenue, and many other things. Think of "setting all your information free" instead of only showing it by month or quarterly. It works, and your colleagues will love it.

Most entrepreneurs enjoy being able to make decisions without long processes. Meetings, bureaucracy, and fear of making decisions is for the politicians and their civil servants, so many entrepreneurs become frustrated when new and more employees, customers, projects, problems and possibilities constantly needs to be discussed in long meetings instead of just being solved. You can actually continue to hold on to this strategy ... even if you become 1-200- or 300. I have tried it. It's just daring to do it and sticking with it!

The talented entrepreneur tackles this by outsourcing certain functions, hiring skilled employees, and ensuring open information and dialogue, but also by being very conscious of one's own role as a leader (and not the boss). Give people the real power of decision, don't participate in all projects and discussions, and thus accept mistakes and failures. And it is important that in a culture where it's OK to fail ... just to know that we should just not repeat mistakes. It is more important to "do something" than to "do nothing".

You can't grow a business if you are involved in all customer negotiations, projects and new initiatives. If you use more than 50% of your time on internal meetings, you are already well on your way to becoming the stop block more than the dynamo for growth.

Besides clear decision-making skills, simple reporting and procedures for email and information sharing, it's also smart to have a clear position for meetings.

Start meetings on time, having stand-up meetings, clear agendas and end times are good meeting practices. Personally, I appreciate walking meetings where the meeting takes place walking outside the office, where the combination of fresh air, a new framework, and informality often provide better and faster discussions. In E-conomic, we also tried having all meetings with only 2-3 participants as walking meetings.

Generally, you can't change who you are, regardless of whether it is a startup or a larger company. Once an entrepreneur, always an entrepreneur, and you should not change your personality and values just to grow or perform a new function.

However, one should self-evaluate as the company grows, assess how best to serve the company, and how you can thrive in the fast-growing enterprise.

You could possibly be the best seller, the best product owner, and the best motivator; but not the best leader. Successful entrepreneurs must always consider whether their role is best outside the top executive chair or, for example, as responsible for product development, sales, export, or innovative projects, and leave the strategic and growth-focusing role to others.

And then there is the Ugly Baby Syndrome. You can be an entrepreneur or even the perfect entrepreneur and leader, but maybe not the best owner. Just as new parents do not see that a newborn baby is ugly, and guests with big smiles call the newborn charming and beautiful, the dominant entrepreneur is at risk of not being able to see errors or defects in their baby/business and not having employees who dare to be critical. Without comparison and without having to sound dramatic, it is important that managers can and dare to "kill your darlings" if the need arises.

New eyes, new forces, and new money through new (co-)owners can often be the critical step in creating the right conditions for growth, so be always open to new ownership structure.

Finally, there is always the rule that you can't forget to get rich ... or is there? There are very healthy ways to shape your company to be dominant and to be the next in the family dynasty, but it happens only for a few. Remember to cash out if the right opportunity arises, if your entrepreneur's spirit is crying out for new start-up activities, or if the right offer comes.

But absolutely essential is that there must be a meaning in what you do/create/build ... besides making money. Remember it. You can't just go to work to earn money. It will not last.

There must be a meaning.

A true entrepreneur is not afraid of the unknown or whether there will be new opportunities. I am the eternal entrepreneur ... for better or for worse. I can't help but be engaged when I meet dedicated, open minded people with ambitious, respectful ideas, that also know how to have fun.

Entrepreneurship and service is everything ... just do it.

JEFF CORNWALL
The rules of bootstrapping a new business

Jeff Cornwall has spent more than forty years as a serial entrepreneur and teacher of entrepreneurs. In the 1970's he started several small businesses and was involved in various family ventures. In the late 1980's, following several years in academia, Dr. Cornwall co-founded Atlantic Behavioral Health Systems in Raleigh, NC and spent nearly a decade leading the company as President/CEO. After growing to more than 300 employees, he and his partners sold most of their healthcare holdings. After the sale, Dr. Cornwall decided it was time to return to the classroom to share his experience and knowledge with aspiring entrepreneurs. Dr. Cornwall remains active as an entrepreneur with the digital content venture he co-founded in 2014, Entrepreneurial Mind, LLC.

Recent studies find that the average business startup has only $6,500-$10,000 in initial capital. So how do entrepreneurs get businesses off the ground with such meager means? They succeed by using a variety of tools and techniques that are known collectively as bootstrapping.

Through the use of bootstrapping, the entrepreneur creatively finds ways to launch and grow a business within the limited resources available to most new ventures. They find ways to achieve what needs to get accomplished for the business by creatively getting it done for a lower cost. There are four key rules to effectively bootstrap a business.

Rule #1: Overhead matters
The first rule of bootstrapping a business is that overhead matters.

Overhead expenses are those fixed costs that happen every month whether you sell anything or not. It can include staff salaries, rent, loan payments, leases, cell phone bills, and so forth.

Bootstrapping some of these costs can help get to breakeven sooner. And the sooner a business reaches breakeven, the sooner it is able to pay the entrepreneur. Breakeven occurs when gross profit (revenue less operating expenses) is enough to cover fixed expenses. If a business makes a profit of $2 after paying for materials and labor to make a product, and its overhead is $10,000 per month, it has to sell 5,000 units to break even. If your overhead can be lowered to $5,000, it only takes sales of 2,500 units a month to break even.

There are a number of steps that can be used to cut overhead during start-up. Keep salaried staff to as few people as possible. Entrepreneurs should try to do as many of the key functions themselves as possible. Rather than hire a full-time bookkeeper, buy simple accounting software to keep the books. Be ready to do simple tasks for as long as possible. In the morning a bootstrapping entrepreneur might be sending out invoices, in the afternoon calling on potential clients, and at night cleaning the office bathrooms. It is also important to keep facility costs as low as possible. Entrepreneurs do this by running the business out of their homes, out of coffee shops, or by borrowing or sharing space.

It is critical to think carefully before committing to any additional fixed monthly expenses. Every time the entrepreneur adds more fixed expenses, you raise the level of sales required to break even.

A note of caution – do not strangle your ability to grow in the quest to bootstrap the business. The goal is to be both efficient and effective. Be frugal, but with a purpose.

Rule #2: Marketing matters

Even though money is tight for small businesses, getting the word out to potential customers is essential if the business is to grow and thrive. The first step in becoming a successful bootstrap marketer is to remember that the impact of the message is more important than its "volume". Unlike a big corporation that can saturate the market with expensive advertising, entrepreneurs often only have a limited set of opportunities to connect with potential customers and communicate their message.

To be successful at this, entrepreneurs must know exactly where their customers go for information. Learn to think like the customer. If they go to social media to find information about products and services, be engaged with social media. If not, then don't bother pushing out information through Twitter and Facebook. Entrepreneurs need to put time and money toward promoting their businesses where their customers actually go to look for information, be it websites, radio ads, and so forth. The message should always be directed toward the business's specific market niche.

Word of mouth would seem to be the ultimate way to engage in bootstrap marketing. However, word of mouth rarely just happens. It takes a deliberate plan to assure that people have a reason to tell others about a business. And it may take some marketing dollars to prime the word of mouth process. For example, incentives to existing customers for referring new business can often be a very effective way to build word of mouth. Social media can help spread word of mouth, but make sure that the message everyone is spreading is the intended message! Word of mouth can be hard to manage and control.

Finally, too many entrepreneurs engage in "panic marketing". They only spend money on marketing when business is soft, thinking that will save them money. However, studies clearly show that "panic marketing" is less effective and more expensive than a patient, steady approach. Marketing should be viewed as a process, not an event.

Rule #3: Employees are single biggest cost

For most small businesses, employee expenses are the highest single cost. To help keep control over cash flow, the entrepreneur should keep a careful eye on payroll expenses and consider some bootstrapping techniques related to human resources.

Entrepreneurs often try to hire people in advance of growth, assuming that it is better to have employees already in place when new business comes in. But this can put a significant strain on cash flow, as you are trying to carry more people on payroll than your current sales can support. One alternative is to engage in employee "stretching". Postpone hiring until sales growth actually happens.

This requires that you get all of your employees on board. Be open and honest. Assure them that although they can anticipate an additional workload in the short run, as soon as sales hit a certain level more people will be hired. Offer some perks, such as additional time off or added profit sharing, as a reward for their willingness to "stretch". Make sure you deliver what you promise, or you will lose credibility and jeopardize their cooperation in the future.

Another common bootstrapping tool for controlling employee costs is to use independent contractors. This way the business only uses people for specific tasks when demand and workload warrant. One caution with this technique is that there are specific legal definitions as to who can be considered an independent contractor.

Hiring student interns is another way to keep employment costs under control. Interns are willing to work for modest pay as they are seeking experience and often will work for free if they get course credit for their work. There are ways that an entrepreneur can use bootstrapping to effectively compete with larger companies to attract management talent. Entrepreneurs can offer managers equity compensation, such as stock options, phantom stock and profit sharing. These types of compensation help postpone high pay to the time when the business can afford it.

Rule #4: Reduce operating costs

Operating costs include salaries and wages, raw material costs and the cost of any facilities that go directly toward producing the product or providing the service. Bootstrapping operating costs through outsourcing can help you get to breakeven sooner and improve profit margins as the business grows. Outsourcing is a strategy that can work very well for startup and very small businesses. Rather than bear the cost of renting space and hiring a staff, these businesses utilize the excess capacity of someone else's business to make their product.

For example, many upscale coffee shops outsource the roasting of coffee beans to a larger producer. They contract with a roaster, or sometimes another coffee shop with a roaster, to supply them with freshly roasted beans as they need them to meet demand. This way the coffee shop owner does not have to buy their own roaster, pay the wages of an employee with those skills, and pay the for the added space that the roaster would require in their store. Outsourcing can usually offer lower per-unit costs for small businesses. Since you are paying for another business's excess capacity, you can take advantage of lower costs they have created through their large volume.

Outsourcing to vendors in low-cost countries can also be a source of savings in operating costs. Just make sure to understand the actual total costs of using international outsourcing opportunities.

Never stop bootstrapping

Bootstrapping is not just for startups. Bootstrapping over the long term helps keep the business efficient, which reduces the need to secure external financing. This allows the entrepreneur to keep ownership of the business, reduces the need for taking on debt, and helps strengthen the business during the current recession. In addition, continuing to bootstrap helps build a stronger cash flow. And the stronger the cash flow, the higher the value of a private business. Bootstrapping, therefore, helps build wealth for the entrepreneur by increasing the value of the venture as it grows.

LISA BØNSDORFF DALSGAARD
See the opportunities in the distractions

Lisa Bønsdorff Dalsgaard is the founder of the Danish co-working space StartupWorks, the woman behind GoodiePack.com, and the Co-founder of MarketLeap, a company that helps startups with their go-to-market strategy.

I believe there are different degrees of being an entrepreneur. The highest level is a successful entrepreneur – someone who has created a well-known concept and a good business. That's the degree that most of us strive towards. One of the greatest challenges on the route to that goal is focus. In the following I'll give you my tools and strategies that help me keep my focus and see the possibilities in the distractions.

Opportunities get me out of bed in the morning

Possibility, the English word for the Danish word *mulighed*, is not defined in the well-known reference website BusinessDictionary.com, which reaches more than 5 million people a month. *Opportunity* is defined as:

Exploitable set of circumstances with uncertain outcome, requiring commitment of resources and involving exposure to risk. In other words, *possibility* implies *risk*. Oddly enough, their definition of risk doesn't contain the word *possibilities*. The same applies to the national Danish reference website, DenStoreDanske.dk, where you find *risiko*, the Danish word for risk, but where the word *mulighed* is not clearly defined. Why? Have we used too little time on possibilities?

Long and challenging discussions may be had about the relationships between possibility, chance and risk, with negative and/or positive charges. For me, possibilities is a positively-charged word, which can have a positive or a negative outcome. When you choose to look at the possibilities, there is still a risk that you may perhaps not reach the vision, or worse. If you look at the risk, there is in return almost always a possibility – at least when I look. Thus for me, possibilities and risks have the same content and outcome – it all depends on how you view the circumstances. I always try to take the opportunistic view, as that gives me a far better workday. Believe in myself and believe that things will succeed!

Why is there no fuller definition of the word possibility? Have we underestimated it? And why don't we learn more about possibilities? How do we see them? How do we grasp them? How do we get from the possibility to the outcome, the positive vision?

Why have I chosen to dedicate my contribution to possibilities?

I believe that a true entrepreneur is one who sees possibilities rather than problems. It is this focus on possibilities rather than risks that means that we dare take the plunge, in the belief that we can go all the way to the positive vision.

Possibilities can be expensive distractions

It is my experience that an entrepreneur with a 'possibilities' character trait is always full of good ideas – and is itching to turn those ideas into reality. If he or she can feel the pressure of scaling up the existing business, then it is really easier for them to see the possibilities in one of the many other ideas and instead start realising one of them. To make matters worse, getting involved in distractions often feels great. They come quite automatically when the desk is littered with bills, registrations and other paperwork, so keeping focused on the strategic work, which is essential to the business, is really a challenge.

The many possibilities and new business ideas can generally be unbelievably distracting in the working day, and apart from thoughts such as these you're also distracted by notifications, messages, emails, telephone calls etc. Gloria Mark, a researcher at the University of California, Irvine, has discovered that a typical office worker only has 11 minutes between each interruption, while it takes an average of 25 minutes to get back to the original task after an interruption. Quite thought-provoking. And according to the Carnegie Mellon University's Human-Computer Interaction Lab, interruptions make us more stupid. Brain researchers debate the impact of gadgets on the brain and on our multi-tasking abilities. The early results show what we already know: when you do several things at the same time, all the efforts suffer, because changing from one task to another comes at a cost. That's something we know very well when we move house, change a subscription or change a supplier. But when the brain changes between tasks or thoughts, measuring the costs is more difficult.

Train your grasping techniques and let the distractions come

We know that distractions are almost unavoidable, but few people know how to use the distractions to their own advantage. Alessandro Acquisti, Professor of Information Technology, and psychologist Eyal Peer at the Carnegie

Mellon University, decided to design an experiment to test the brain during interruptive distractions, and they discovered something unexpected.

They invited 136 people to their laboratory and asked them to read a text and answer questions about it. One group was to complete the task without interruptions, while the members of a second group were told that they might be given additional instructions by text messages while carrying out the task. They were interrupted twice by text messages. Acquisti and Peer started a new test and asked all the participants to read and answer questions, but this time the group that was interrupted before was divided into two, and only the members of one of these two groups were interrupted, although the members of both groups expected interruptions. In the first part of the experiment, the group that was interrupted made 20% more errors than the group that was not interrupted. In the second part of the experiment, the group that was interrupted also performed worse than the group that was not interrupted, but they made only 14% more errors. The researchers' explanation was that people who expect to be interrupted can learn to improve their way of tackling the task.

The most interesting aspect, however, was that the group that had been warned that it might be interrupted, but wasn't interrupted, showed a 43% improvement and actually outperformed the group that was never interrupted. This was a completely unexpected discovery and shows, according to the researchers, that the participants learned from their experience and adapted their brains to the situation. They were thus successful in exploiting their brain capacity even better to withstand an interruption, and the researchers' explanation was that the potential interruption may have given them a deadline that made them even more focused on completing the task.

So you can train yourself to tackle distraction, even when you don't know when the distraction comes.

So what can the entrepreneur learn from this research? Precisely that interruptions are costly, but experience and deadlines can generate so much focus that you can reach a higher level. Experience is training, so here are a couple of other tools that I use to see possibilities in distractions:

This is how you train …
1. The pattern in entrepreneurs' procrastination activities
I have a little black book, an idea book. For me the value is not in the book itself, but in an act: What happens when I write my new business ideas in the book, is that I prioritise, I focus.

When I look in my book, I can see old ideas that I can laugh at today. I see ideas that others have turned into reality. Ideas that have been overtaken by the modern world, and ideas that still have potential. Most of all I learn a great deal from looking in my black book. I can actually see a pattern in the branches of business and the types of idea I get. Typically, I get ideas in media and marketing and, primarily, in new ways into existing markets. Therefore, I know, word for word, which branches I'm passionate about, and I am better able to keep on track.

2. The Hemingway Bridge

In his book Disciplined Dreaming: A Proven System to Drive Breakthrough Creativity, Josh Linkner writes about his favourite technique, the Hemingway Bridge, which is used to avoid the problem of stopping and starting. Rather than ending a chapter and then beginning the next day with a blank page, Ernest Hemingway would write the first paragraph of the next chapter before ending his days' work. Having already put the initial thoughts on the page allowed him to pick up midstream rather than from a dead stop. It works. When customers call GoodiePack, or when there's a knock on my door at our entrepreneurial manor house, I use the first few seconds to start a new sentence in my writing – without using a full stop. Then it's easier for me to return to my writing and perhaps even see new opportunities when I continue the sentence.

3. Exploit creative distractions

Generally, it's my creativity that distracts me most in my working day. My creativity generates new business ideas. So I must be proactive and use my creativity in the existing business. That's why I draw trees. I draw a tree of markets, where each branch indicates a new market. I draw trees for income channels, marketing channels and for the technical business development. I'll happily draw a whole forest of trees to get an overview. Each tree has roots, a trunk, branches, shoots and leaves, which shows me the steps I must go through before I can harvest the fruits as a successful entrepreneur.

There are opportunities every time you get distracted. You can choose to drop the unfinished work in order to start something new, or drop the unfinished work, reverting to it later to discover opportunities. You can train by starting to accept that as an entrepreneur you cannot avoid distractions - instead you should grasp them and know how to deal with the opportunities they represent. The more you train, the more experience you get. That's how you find your focus.

DAVID HEINEMEIER HANSSON
The stoic way

David Heinemeier Hansson is the creator of Ruby on Rails, founder & CTO at Basecamp (formerly 37signals), best selling author, Le Mans class-winning racing driver, public speaker, hobbyist photographer and family man.

There's an exhilarating freedom and motivation in having nothing to lose. History is full of amazing tales of underdog ingenuity. Likewise, stereotypes abound of the mighty falling flat, trying desperately to protect what they've got.

But even more insidious than actively trying to protect what you have, is frequent fretting about how to do so in your mind. It's so easy to fall into an endless churn of worries about how your precious gains could vanish tomorrow.

This is known as loss aversion. It's the default routing of our evolutionary brains, and it can lead to unnecessary stress, lost opportunities and poor decision-making. But it doesn't have to be your destiny – it is indeed possible to reroute.

The stoic practice of negative visualization is one way to do this. If you imagine, clearly and frequently, the worst case scenario, you can work on coming to terms with its consequences. Usually they're far less dire than your worries would lead you to believe.

I've employed this technique from the get-go with everything I hold dear in my life. As an example, here's how I've applied this to the thought that a terrible end could prematurely doom Basecamp.

It's easy to contemplate all sorts of spectacular ways this could happen: A massive hack that destroys all data, all backups. Some sort of epic fraud that indicts the entire company. I let my mind seek out all sorts of terrible corners.

Then I consider what's left: I got to work with amazing people for over a decade. I grew as a programmer, as a manager, and as a business person immensely. I enjoyed most days, most of the time. I helped millions of people be more productive doing all sorts of wonderful things.

I'm so much better off for having been through this, regardless of how a possible end might occur for the company. This makes whether circumstances allow us to continue for another decade (or five!) a lesser deal than the fact that we did for one.

This brings a calmness, a tranquility, as the stoics would say, that's incredibly liberating. A head free of fear or dread. I believe this not only is a saner, healthier way to live (stress wrecks havoc on the body and soul), but also better for the company.

We're not running Intel, and I don't want to have Grove's "only the paranoid survive" as my modus operandi. I want to retain the underdog sense of having nothing to lose, even when conventional thought might say I (and the company) have everything to lose.

That's the tranquil freedom of the stoic way.

CHIP CONLEY
From entrepreneur to CEO

Hotel guru. Armchair psychologist. Traveling philosopher. Author. Speaker. Teacher. Student.

Why are entrepreneurs loved and CEO's hated? It's a bit of irony that has not been lost on me this past week, as a bunch of cyber-strangers weighed in on their perception of me based upon a photo. Is this a crazy entrepreneur or a CEO who has lost his mind and proper bearings?

Back in June, the Rasmussen Reports released a survey of Americans' favorable vs. unfavorable ratings of various professions. At the top of the list with almost no negativity were small business owners and entrepreneurs. Religious leaders were a fair percentage back, but still near the top. Bankers were evenly loved and hated, while journalists, lawyers and stockbrokers started to make up the bottom of the list. But, in the valley of the despised were CEO's and Members of Congress. Three times as many people give these two professions negative ratings as compared to the positives.

So, what happens when you start out as an entrepreneur, but grow into being a CEO due to the success of your company? Is Steve Jobs an entrepreneur or a CEO? How about Richard Branson? So much of it has to do with how you show up – are you still yourself, or have you become the empty, shifty "suit"? Well, I started my company almost two dozen years ago as sort of an artist entrepreneur, and I've been getting "atta boys" along the way. Yet, when I showed up in the Nevada desert to enjoy a few days of artistic utopia at Burning Man, had a few pics taken of me, and then posted them on my Facebook account, the question of whether I was a wacky entrepreneur or a father figure CEO made me a cause celebre the past few days. Take a look at the blog I wrote for BNET and the nearly 150 comments that arose from this topical question, how much of a CEO's personal life should we be exposed to? (link: http://www.bnet.com/2403-13058_23-358555.html)

What's most fascinating is to read that those who championed my right to be myself saw me as a grown-up entrepreneur, but those who thought I'd crossed the line by posting my Burning Man photos to my private Facebook account saw me as the CEO who had a certain decorum of professionalism that I needed to maintain (even though, frankly, that sterile decorum may be one of the reasons why Americans score CEO's so low). One of those who counseled me on being a little more professional, writes as if he were a self-hating CEO, "As much as you may not enjoy it, being a CEO brings with it the serious responsibilities of being a parental role model." Clearly, this parental thing ain't working, based upon the Rasmussen results. More encouraging were the comments like "I am glad to see someone can be successful and not turn into a soulless robot" or "how refreshing it is to see a CEO who is also a human."

One common comment was that I should separate my friends from my business associates on my Facebook page and only let my friends into that part of my site that might have photos like this. I don't know what century they're living in, but many of us – especially those who work long hours in business – find that some of our closest friends are those we connect with during our business day. This work/life frappe has created a blended experience in which it is harder than ever to compartmentalize. Thank God ... we may put a few shrinks out of business, but we're likely to be a whole lot happier. Public image should equal private reality.

Ironically, my first book's subtitle was "Daring to be Yourself in Business," and I'm seeing how vital that is in the age of transparency. With the internet and social networks taking a more prominent place in our lives, being true to yourself (and everyone else) is almost a requirement. In fact, I'd suggest that the Rasmussen poll is really a litmus test for authenticity. The more people see the participants in the profession as authentic, the more heroic they become in the eyes of the public. Authenticity is where the culture is headed. It's an evolutionary process (coincidentally, the theme of this last year's Burning Man was "Evolution"). And, I'm still just figuring out my evolutionary process of gravitating from being an entrepreneur to being a CEO. Yet, this experience has just reinforced a powerful lesson. Maybe the role model CEO I'm supposed to be isn't the traditional icon that people don't like and don't trust, but it's the CHO: the Chief Human Officer. That's really the conundrum a modern-age role model CEO must solve: how can we be human and be a CEO at the same time?

Note: Originally published in 2009.

MADS LANGER
Leaning forward in life

Mads Langer is a Danish singer-songwriter with success both in and outside Denmark.

Singer-songwriter Mads Langer is one of the relatively few Danish artists who has successfully transformed from being a talent into a star with long-term durability in the Danish music heaven. It's a dream that unbelievably many in his generation, and not least those who are younger than Mads, have or have had.

As the editor of this book, I became acquainted with the entrepreneurial way in which Mads thinks and acts in his branch – the music branch. Therefore, I invited him to coffee and a chat about how you run a business when you're a musical entrepreneur, and what 'leaning forward in life' means …

Some people may be surprised to see your name in a book like this one. Do you consider yourself an entrepreneur?

Yes, very much so. Today I lead a business that I started myself and which is driven by art. We've become quite a large team that shares a passion for music, and my role is to be both a leader of and an innovator in Foodsnakes & Co, which is what this business is called.

So you view yourself as both artist and entrepreneur. As a successful entrepreneur you will typically invest some of the success you've achieved in expanding your platform. In other words, think about how you move forward and innovate from the place you've reached. Do you also work as an entrepreneur in that way?

I work with short-, medium- and long-term objectives for my life as an entrepreneur.

Right now I am finalising a medium-term objective that started in 2010, when I signed a contract with Sony in London. We did a deal for three albums and I recently issued the third one, so I'm now in a situation where I must decide what the next chapter of my music life will contain.

Should I continue with Sony, look elsewhere, start my own label or what?

In the short term it's a matter of supporting, in the best possible way, the record I've used two years of my life making. That applies to both my Danish and my international public. My short-term objective is thus success in a large market outside Denmark – Germany, for example. In that connection I'll also be looking at Sony as a multinational company and see how they deliver on the things we've agreed. How much are they willing to invest?

I've made my contribution by building up the German market. For example, I've given a series of concerts that either just paid their way or cost me money. You have to remember that my business is quite a large machine when we're touring. We're 20 people in a double-decker bus and we have to have accommodation, transport, food and drink and so on. So that means that if 1,000 people come to our concert in Cologne, it only just pays for itself, and if we then play for a smaller audience in Bremen, I suddenly start to draw on my capital.

That illustrates very well the degree of entrepreneurship there is in this. It's not the record company that runs the financial risk, it's me.

How can you afford to take all these chances?

That's due to a wonderful customer adviser at a bank, whom I've known since I was a child in Skive (small Danish city). This adviser has known me since I was a little boy, and he's always believed in my talent. So it was a great victory for me to go back to my childhood bank in Skive with a cheque for the DKK 750,000 that they'd loaned me over the years simply because they have faith in my abilities as a musician and entrepreneur.

Something many entrepreneurs find difficult is sales. It can be a problem, as very little in life sells itself. You don't seem like a point-of-a-gun salesman to me ...

No, but I've discovered that I'm really good at meeting new people. I've always been very focused and conscious about what I want and don't want. That approach has had a selling impact on people in the industry, as they could feel that this wasn't just a voice, there was also a personality behind it. As a musical entrepreneur I've had a large talent. You can compare it with other entrepreneurs who have a good idea and some skills to turn that idea into reality. You pitch that idea to an investor, and in the same way I pitched my songs to the record labels ahead of my first album. I went to the five largest record labels in Copenhagen with my demo, and it turned out later that four of them wanted to sign me up.

That pleased me very much, but rather than just saying yes immediately, I used a long time to talk to the different labels and the people behind them. It was important to me to feel where the human 'chemistry' was, and it was also essential for me that they had long-term plans for a possible collaboration.

I sense that you put emphasis on two things in particular when you act as a musical entrepreneur: That authenticity and your heart are in it, but that you also have enough business sense to focus on getting a good and fair deal. Is that right?

It is, in the sense that, when I had my first negotiations with the various record labels, I also tried to play them against each other to get the best offer. But when that's said, it was vital that we had values in common. Therefore, I've always gone after deals that were an investment in the future rather than going for a quick profit. I've never gone after a lot of up-front money, but chose my first record label – Copenhagen Records – because the people behind it were fired up and got high on what they did. They were men of the world and down to earth at the same time, and we saw where each of us was coming from and spoke the same language.

As an entrepreneur, things are ultimately not so much about oneself and far more about one's team – at least if you're a growth entrepreneur and want to create something substantial. In that case you're very dependent on getting the right people around you and getting everything to work together. That also requires leadership in addition to entrepreneurship. Is Mads Langer a good leader as well?

The greatest and most difficult lesson for me has been how to get the right team together. I came into this industry with clear values, some ideals and some visions based on my boyhood dream. But I was very naïve and ignorant regarding the mechanisms in the music industry.

When I look back ten years, to when I really started, I can see that my most important indicator has always been my gut feeling. I've always reminded myself to listen to it in a world where there are very many opinions and cooks.

It's all to do with the fact that what people fall in love with is you. If the music industry changes my fundamental DNA, then that'll destroy my business and ultimately myself. Listening to good suggestions about the directions you can go and the ideas that e.g. my record label had when it was a matter of marketing my music and selling my messages is excellent. But ultimately it's me they've invested in because they believed in me and saw my idea was sustainable.

But I must also be honest and say that it's only now, ten years after my debut, that "the perfect team" is in place. It's been a process of replacing people and testing them, expansions and reductions, and a learning curve in understanding the mechanisms working between people.

Now you're finally making a living with your song-writing and your songs. How does the financial side of a business like yours look?

For me, streaming of my music is a very small part of my total business – just a very few percent. Among other things, that's because the distribution ratio between artists and streaming providers still isn't finalised. We earn far too little on the music.

It's therefore vital in my case to have competent management who can sign sponsorship agreements on my behalf and find good matches between me and the streaming providers that are looking for collaboration, such as the one I have with Danish mobile telephony provider Telmore at the moment.

On the whole, good management is the cornerstone in running a business like mine. My management does a great deal of work for me. They look after my diary and accounts, book my band, venues etc. They're my army, and I regard much of my business as a family business, where my band, crew and management are people I also want to drink a cup of coffee with when I'm taking time off.

How do you work with your product as an entrepreneur? For example, I've read that, for your most recent album, you had written 86 songs that you had to cut down to the 11 songs that were on the issued album. That's very reminiscent of how a typical entrepreneur starts. You believe you've got it absolutely right, but then you experience that things have to be adjusted and a great deal of fat has to be carved away before you can make your mark ...

Like all other forms of entrepreneurship, musical entrepreneurship is a question of tenacity and patience. When I develop my product – i.e. my songs – I have a dogma in my song-writing that I don't want to think analytically. If anyone in the studio mentions the words 'radio single', I throw them out, because creative freedom is completely vital for me.

That said, it is obvious that the songs don't become hits by themselves. Apart from the music, breaking through requires a great deal of money and muscle, as you have to invest in adverts, rounds of interviews, well-known bloggers who must be paid, TV campaigns and the like.

In classic entrepreneurship we have the TV program 'Dragons' Den', where you can pitch your business idea in the hope of attracting investment finance and expertise. 'The X Factor' has long been a concept in the music industry. What do you think about it – is it a good path to tread if, like you, one has a dream of being able to live from one's musical talent?

I don't think that 'The X Factor' has anything to do with my branch of the music industry. In my eyes it is essential that you are self-sufficient as a musician before you look for help in the industry. By that I mean that you must have a finished idea and an idea about your own artistic DNA before you contact a record label and pitch your idea.

If that process takes five years, then it takes five years. On the way it can be a really good idea to contact artists who are better established and learn from them, but that's not really what happens in 'The X Factor'.

'The X Factor' is entertainment, where you sell a dream, and as entertainment it is fun to watch, and I can also be moved by it. So my answer shouldn't be understood to mean I'm opposed to 'The X Factor', but I don't regard the program as a serious player in my game.

For me the key is not found in the need for a quick fix if you're serious about wanting to live from making music. You mustn't do it for the fix, but because you can't stop yourself. It would be really stupid to go into the music business to get rich and be famous, as it's only 0.1 percent of us who can actually make money doing it. For me the best way to say it is that it's the same thing that made me happy when I went to the little music school in Skive way back then. It's the love of music. Nothing else.

No matter whether you dream of living from music, as you did as a boy, or you consider becoming an entrepreneur in a completely different industry, what have you learnt that you'd like to pass on to other aspiring entrepreneurs?

Perhaps my most important approach to life as an entrepreneur and a human being is never, ever, let your fears control you. It's a matter of leaning forward in life. Not taking decisions based on a fear of what can go wrong. In other words, as a human being and an entrepreneur, live life progressively rather than regressively.

I'm in a place where people have found my voice and I've found people who listen. That's something I wish for all entrepreneurs, and as long as you make an effort every day, know your own limits and strengths, then I'm sure that you'll probably reach some of your dreams and targets.

THERE IS ONLY ONE WAY
TO AVOID CRITICISM:
DO NOTHING, SAY NOTHING,
AND BE NOTHING.

Aristotle

THOR THORØE
Only dead fish go with the flow

Thor Thorøe is a social entrepreneur and has started businesses such as Paradis is, CocoaFair and Social Foodies.

To be born in the yellow room – a definition of a child of two parents who both work outside the home and who are therefore out every day from morning to evening – automatically gives you a good starting point as an entrepreneur. That was in the period from the late 1970s to the early 1980s, when school finished at 1.30 pm at the latest, and when the rest of the day was spent getting enough good ideas to avoid total boredom.

I didn't have many friends at school, so I invented three new ones: Javre, Die and Drae. They were the ones who gave me the ability to take the plunge as an entrepreneur two decades later. I've used 12,600 hours alone together with my 'friends' – time enough to be creative and think outside the box. As I was the only one among my 'friends' who could make real decisions, the path from idea to action wasn't long.

To date I have started numerous businesses, which have either been divested and afterwards run by others, closed because of bad execution, or are part of a current concept. But what has characterised them all is that the time from idea to planning the concepts was less than an hour.

The new entrepreneur gene

In relation to other historic human races, Homo sapiens is the socially aware entrepreneur who thinks horizontally in and around his business sphere. He isn't satisfied with just generating financial profit for himself and the business's shareholders. The modern entrepreneur thinks in broad terms and about how his products and services can solve social challenges such as pollution, stress, economic inequality and better quality of life for society's disadvantaged.

Politicians talk of the need to create more growth companies that can create jobs and draw foreign currency to the country. What if half of the employees in the growth company buckle and go under because of stress? It could be that the taxes and duties and a positive trade balance suddenly become a bad deal for Denmark.

We live in a protected welfare state that produces employees rather than entrepreneurs. It's no surprise that many entrepreneurs go under during their first years. We need older, committed souls (in their late 20s and their 30s, please), but most of them are so comfortable in their middle-management functions, with regular, monthly salaries and pensions, that they won't risk a life as an entrepreneur without a safety net that can catch them if they fall.

It will take time – perhaps generations – to further develop the world's present-day entrepreneurs.

It's been shown that, 40,000-50,000 years ago, the Neanderthals interbred and shared environments on Earth with what became the Homo sapiens of today. This "cloning" of two human races has meant a stronger immune system for the survivors, but we know the historic development – the Neanderthals were extinct over time.

Tomorrow's entrepreneur must therefore think deeply and broadly about which products and services tomorrow's world citizens will want.

There's at least one good reason why the value of today's businesses making healthy products is rated higher than the value of the companies selling unhealthy products. Consumers increasingly want products that reflect their dreams and lifestyles.

There are three things in particular that entrepreneurs must think about when they are developing their business ideas. In the following I have used two Danish businesses that I have built up as examples.

What are the concept's distinctive characteristics?
What is it that makes your concept/product unique – both today and tomorrow? In other words, how do you differentiate yourself from your direct and indirect competitors? Apart from your characteristics, which unique selling points (USPs) ensure that it's easier for you to attract capital, the most competent staff, the sales contracts etc.?

When I started the Paradis is ice cream chain back in 2000, what was special about me was that I had been to Italy and had brought old ice cream recipes back with me. I used these recipes to develop the freshest freshly-made ice cream on the market, which gave the customers a unique taste experience. I knew it was only a matter of time before the concept was copied, as the distinctive feature was easy to imitate. We therefore decided in 2004 to turn Paradis is into a franchise concept, so the development of the outlet concept could explode.

Today, the business has lost its distinctiveness because no work has been done strategically and in a targeted way to maintain the good position that it had on the ice cream market.

Social Foodies was founded in 2012 and had its starting point in the almost four years I spent in Africa, where my prime task was to build up a watertight distinctive characteristic: to help small farmers in Africa get a better life. I set up two businesses in South Africa and Mozambique. Both businesses were aimed at giving me two very vital ingredients for my future concept in Denmark: (1) good, cheap raw materials and (2) a lot of credible and unique human stories that have made a marked difference to the individual.

How relevant is your concept for your target group?

Through how many sales and distribution channels will you be able to offer your products? The businesses that don't survive the competition are those that cannot build up a solid position for themselves in e-commerce. You will also be able to achieve a considerable competitive advantage if you can supply products to both the B2C and B2B markets simultaneously. A second parameter, which many people forget, is to ask, How relevant is your product during the day, the month or the year? Selling Christmas trees in the summer is difficult. On the other hand, if you're known for selling lunches, then you're perhaps not exploiting the full potential during the rest of the day or week.

Paradis is faces a large challenge, as the business's main product is so well known that people don't connect the concept with anything other than ice cream. That means there is only activity in the chain's outlets eight months of the year; the rest of the time the chain is invisible to customers. That makes the chain vulnerable if new concepts appear with a broader palette of seasonal products.

Ice cream as a category is particularly vulnerable, as you can't send it by mail, and building up an economically sustainable B2B department is only possible to a limited extent, as transport again makes this impossible.

In Social Foodies we also have a challenge in that our products are primarily relevant to our customers at weekends and on special occasions, when people want to indulge themselves (ice cream, however, is also relevant on weekdays in the summer months). Instead of expanding the product mix to include everyday products, we've changed our way of organising our staff and production. The weekdays are now used to make products for all sales channels while using fewer staff.

Social Foodies' great advantage is in its coverage of all sales channels, from courses for private consumers and businesses to sales in shops and online, and to sales of products to businesses.

Value for many versus value for money

Many new entrepreneurs – and even established businesses – focus on giving the customer greater value for money. That's OK in itself, but it is a very narrow, egoistic way of thinking. Our welfare state is under enormous pressure and there's a need for thinking up creative solutions to prevent a total collapse. Unfortunately, politicians only think four years ahead to the next election, not the 20 years that would serve society and its citizens better. But that gives visionary entrepreneurs a golden opportunity to develop products and services that can help the welfare state.

In Social Foodies we've decided to include social innovation among our set of values. In 2015 it led to a collaboration with the Thorshøjgaard centre in Ishøj, which primarily helps young people with Asperger's syndrome. Today they pack our boxes of nuts and deliver them to our B2B customers in Greater Copenhagen (Denmark). More than 20 people are involved, and the collaboration is now being expanded to include more products and transporting products between our shops and customers every day. That will double the need for young, socially disadvantaged people. This will be of great benefit to the young people and society, but naturally also for the business and the centre.

When I gave a talk recently, I offered our freshly made muesli bars to some representatives of the public sector, at DKK 1 each, instead of the normal price of DKK 20. They smiled broadly, accepted my offer and ordered 100 bars for their department.

Later, I returned to these representatives and gave them an invoice for DKK 2,000. Seeing the strange look on their faces, I hastily explained that they were representatives of society, and given that the price of the muesli bars to society was DKK 1 each, not DKK 20, I'd already saved the public sector (their local authority) DKK 19 for each bar because their vulnerable young people had been activated.

If you want to stand out from the crowd, become a social entrepreneur. Remember, it's only dead fish that go with the flow.

TANIA ELLIS
Do good & do well:
Give while you grow!

Tania Ellis is a Danish-British prize-winning writer, speaker and business innovator, specialized in social business trends and strategies. Her expertise and hands-on involvement in blending economic and social value with business strategy and innovation has made her a popular inspirational speaker and strategic advisor with clients ranging from entrepreneurial companies to large international corporate brands.

What makes you rich?

If I asked you what it is that makes you rich, what would you answer?

Maybe you'd mention your annual income or savings. But you might also mention the time spent with your family, your good health, or time spent in nature. In other words, you have several bottom lines in your life.

The same goes for business. At least for those who believe in the new business logic, where financial performance and social responsibility go hand in hand.

Here, the goal is not to ensure economic growth at the expense of the environment or people's well-being. It's about creating sustainable growth by creating value for society as well as the company's financial bottom line.

Does this sound like hippie nonsense? Perhaps there was a time when it was.

Hello social capitalism!

The era where the sole purpose of business was to generate profit and value for its owners, while public institutions, NGO's and engaged citizens watched over society's interests, is now over.

Today the business environment is much more complex, and expectations from employees and other stakeholders much more demanding. The world has grown smaller, the effects of our unsustainable behavior more visible, and people's awareness of this higher than ever.

That's why companies today have to do good and do well. Say hello to social capitalism.

The business case

It's not (only) morality and ethics that drive the new business logic. Corporate social responsibility is becoming a competitive parameter on line with price and quality.

Today, companies operate in a world where global issues like resource scarcity, social inequality, and the threat of global warming can affect production costs, preferred supplier status and more.

And so, many companies around the world – from Maersk and LEGO to Nike and Unilever – are in the course of integrating sustainability and responsibility into their core business and daily operations.

To some companies, corporate sustainability and responsibility (CSR) is all about risk management, and during the last couple of years convincing business cases for risk-focused CSR have emerged.

For example, a recent study (ESG – a new equity factor, Nykredit, 2014) of 5,000 global, listed companies' performances showed that those who were in control of their social and environmental risks had twice as high a return as those who were not.

Other studies show that the value of incorporating social responsibility as part of the business include important contributions to the company's top and bottom line, such as a strong image, preferred supplier status, optimized operational performance, higher employee engagement, stronger customer relations.

In short, it pays off to give back.

Profit & purpose

Society's challenges and needs have not only become business opportunities. Business has also become an important means for creating new solutions that address society's challenges and needs.

Enter the social entrepreneurs, who are transforming corporate social responsibility into corporate social innovation with sustainable solutions that make a profit as well as a positive difference in the world.

Like the Danish social business Specialisterne, an IT company with a business based on the particular competencies that people with autism have.

The company's business model – and the employment potential that it entails – is so unique that Specialisterne today has become an international success with branches in more than 13 countries. It has even become a business case at Harvard Business School.

Or like the sustainable children's clothes company VIGGA, which has built a circular service design business model by offering organic high-quality children's clothes on subscription.

Once the child outgrows the clothes, VIGGA replaces it with new clothes that fit, and the returned clothes are laundered and made ready for the next family, who can reduce their environmental footprint by up to 80%. In 2015, the company won the international Sustainia Award for providing the world's most sustainable solution in the fashion industry.

Specialisterne and VIGGA are just two examples of the growing movement of socially conscious impact entrepreneurs that have emerged worldwide over the past decades. Just like d.Light (sells solar-powered lamps in countries where people lack electricity), Aravind Eye Care System (provides eye care services to the rural poor), TerraCycle (a worldwide leader in the collection and repurposing of hard-to-recycle post-consumer waste, from used chip bags to used cigarette butts). And many, many more.

To these companies, social responsibility is not about risk management or a nice-to-have add-on to the core business. It is the very purpose of their business to contribute positively to society's sustainable development goals.

You can also Give & Grow!
You can also be a social capitalist, and give back to society while you still grow your business. No matter the size of your company or industry you're in.

Here are some relatively simple ways to get started:
- Volunteer your professional skills in support of a good cause

- Donate part of your sales to charity

- Select suppliers and business partners that support sustainable development goals

- Invest in social businesses or sustainable development projects

- Buy office supplies and other products with a green or social profile.

You could also create a closer link between your business and responsibility efforts. Here are five examples of how:
- Is one of your business goals to cut operating costs? Then it might make sense to focus on energy-saving or recycling solutions.

- Is your biggest business challenge to attract and retain talent? Then see how you could involve your employees in corporate responsibility efforts and link this to your employer branding.

- Are you planning to move your production overseas? Then putting an effort into responsible supply chain management could give you a competitive advantage.

- Could any of your company values be related to CSR? If a key value is, say, innovation, this could be linked to developing products or services with a green or social profile.

- Is competition tough in your industry, or do you need to revitalize your business? Then make a review of UN's 17 Sustainable Development Goals (SDGs) and see which ones you could align with in order to differentiate your business efforts.

If you're really, really ambitious, you could even challenge the very vision and mission or your company by asking: Why are we here – what is our purpose? What kind of (social) value do or can we create with our business? What kind of financial and social impact do we want to make both short and long term? And why?

As you can see, there are so many ways to get started. My personal and professional experience from working in the field for more than a decade has showed me again and again that once you start looking at your business through the "Give & Grow" lens, you discover many exciting new business and development opportunities that can help you both do good and do well. Giving back while you grow is not only about good karma. It also makes good business sense to do so.

FREDERIK OTTESEN
Little Sun – from little things big things grow

Frederik Ottesen is an experienced entrepreneur with a background in mechanical engineering and economics. A strong believer in sustainable technologies, Ottesen works closely alongside Solar Flight's engineers and aviators in realising the company's new projects, such as the world's first passenger-carrying solar-powered airplane – now flying – and a larger solar-powered utility aircraft currently in development. He is the former CEO of Matriks A/S, a software company he started in 1998.

In 2012 he co-founded Little Sun together with artist Olafur Eliasson in order to get clean, reliable, affordable energy to the 1.1 billion people in the world living in off-grid areas without electricity. Little Sun addresses the need for energy in a sustainable way that benefits off-grid communities by working with local entrepreneurs, creating local jobs, and generating local profits.

I founded Little Sun in 2012 with my friend artist Olafur Eliasson, to bring solar energy and business opportunities to as many people as possible, with a particular focus on Sub-Saharan African communities not connected to the electrical grid. We saw first-hand the challenges that result from the lack of reliable, affordable energy in these off-grid areas: people breathing the toxic smoke of kerosene lanterns, students unable to study, along with working hours and income reduced.

Our first solar product, the Little Sun solar lamp, is a little solution that is creating big changes. There are other solar lamps on the market, but Little Sun has a fresh approach in regard to two crucial aspects – design and distribution. Based on the Ethiopian meskel flower, a symbol of positivity and beauty, Little Sun's bright design resulted from feedback we sought and received locally from our key customers in Ethiopia.

Little Sun is a social business, and the way we choose to distribute Little Sun lamps to people in off-grid areas sets us apart from other solar lamps around. Since we also sell Little Suns in on-grid areas (e.g. Europe, the USA, Japan, and Australia), we use this revenue to make the same high-quality lamps available in off-grid areas at locally affordable prices.

As most people are familiar with charity distribution models, I always get asked the question, 'Why don't you just give lamps away for free to people in off-grid areas?' And the answer is simple: because there is no future in that.

If a company gives, for example, 20,000 lamps away to an off-grid community in Sub-Saharan Africa, there is a small benefit immediately, but increasingly diminishing returns. After a few years, the rechargeable batteries in the lamps will reach the end of their lifespan, and what do people do then? The community is back where they started and will either need another donation or will return to using expensive and unhealthy fuel-based lighting.

Instead, we focus on a long-term system that creates a financial infrastructure in off-grid areas by providing great business opportunities. Little Sun works with local entrepreneurs and trains them to sell Little Sun lamps in their off-grid communities – which creates local jobs and generates local profits. And alongside jobs, a sense of pride and hope for the future is generated, as entire communities make the gradual switch to solar – which, as well as being healthier and safer, is a very affordable source of energy. And to make this system accessible to all, we offer an initial stock of lamps on credit, when necessary, in order to kick-start the distribution process.

The benefits of this system are many: after community members' lamps are paid for, they have extra funds as they no longer need to purchase kerosene for light on a daily basis. Sales agents are making income by selling lamps. Just recently in Tanzania, for example, two of our sales agents earned enough by selling lamps to buy their own car – a major achievement. When the batteries in their customers' lamps need to be replaced, sales agents supply and install them, so the same lamps can be used for five to six years.

The Little Sun solar lamp is the first step up the sustainable energy ladder. It is giving many people all over the world – both with electricity and without – their first experience with solar power in a personal, tangible way. Little Sun Charge is the next step up the energy ladder. It's a solar phone charger with an inbuilt lamp which we kick-started in September 2015 through a crowdfunding campaign. People everywhere were incredibly supportive of the project – we crowdfunded more than 500% of our initial goal of 50,000€. In the long run, we plan to launch many more solar products, empowering people all over the world.

What excites me about Little Sun is not only delivering reliable and affordable solar energy, but also the fact that with this energy, we offer great business opportunities to off-grid solar entrepreneurs, making it possible for them to strengthen their communities from within.

I want to see more equality on a global scale. When people in communities without electricity have a clean, reliable, affordable source of energy, the quality of life improves immediately. Children can study. People can make more money. Medical care becomes safer. Families can spend time together around a clean source of light. Little Sun is making this happen. I don't want people to just think about having a greener environment – I want them to do something about it. I want to leave a better world for my children's generation.

To achieve that or any other goal, you need to be passionate about what you do. Create something that matters. I started my software company in 1998. It was a success, but I wanted something that mattered more. That's when I started working with Solar Flight on building the world's first passenger-carrying solar-powered airplane. The Sunseeker DUO moves people or cargo from point A to point B, and when they get to the destination, the airplane has more stored energy than when it started. Both Solar Flight and Little Sun are inspiring the world to become more environmentally conscious. And that is definitely something that matters.

I see opportunity everywhere to do something better than the way it's being done now. And in that moment of inspiration, everything is possible. The critique comes later. Transforming creative ideas into reality requires technical ability, but, most importantly, an unwavering belief in what you want to achieve, no matter how small it may start out.

I'VE LEARNED THAT
PEOPLE WILL FORGET
WHAT YOU SAID,
PEOPLE WILL FORGET
WHAT YOU DID,
BUT PEOPLE WILL NEVER
FORGET HOW YOU
MADE THEM FEEL.

Maya Angelou

SELINA JUUL
Changing the world with entrepreneurship and 30 million views

Selina Juul is Chairman of the Board and Founder of Stop Wasting Food movement Denmark, winner of Nordic Council Nature and Environment Prize 2013, named Dane of the Year 2014, named European Young Leader 2018 and blogger at The Huffington Post.

www.stopwastingfoodmovement.org

"Superheroes don't always wear capes – sometimes they wear aprons," was one of the several thousands of comments on a BBC Facebook video of Selina Juul and her work on the Stop Wasting Food movement. The video was viewed over 30 million times and shared over 150,000 times worldwide. Later that year, CNN also made a video of Selina Juul.

Selina Juul is the founder of Denmark's first and largest NGO against food waste, the Stop Wasting Food movement (Stop Spild Af Mad). Within the last 10 years she managed to turn the entire country's focus on food waste from zero to maximum, she worked with three governments and collaborates with the EU and UN. Recently, she joined the global coalition against food waste, Champions 12.3 with prominent leaders such as CEO of Nestlé, a EU Commissioner and a former White House chef. Selina Juul's work has been featured in over 15,000 press articles in over 40 countries, inspiring people all over the world to take action and stop wasting food. She also did two TEDx Talks and gave speeches at over 300 international conferences and events. Since 2010, Selina has written over 195 articles on food waste in national and international media – and today she writes for The Huffington Post USA.

The editor of this book, Jonathan Løw, was so inspired by Selina's work that he invited Selina to write an article for the book. Since her calendar is almost impossible, the article turned into an interview with focus on a central topic: How can entrepreneurship change the world?

Selina. The research shows that the most influential entrepreneurs in the world are the best survivors. That's pretty much a Charles Darwin theory. Do you think that you are one of these social entrepreneurs?

"If you want to change the world, you have to work hard and you have to stay focused. If you can survive the mental pressure of being exposed 30 million times due to a BBC video daily to receive – and manage to reply to – over 100 requests, to keep your cool while making events with members of the Royal Family, top politicians and prime ministers, to speak on a stage in front of an audience of 7,500 people from 40 countries and to keep your flame burning for a great cause for over 10 years – then yes, I am definitely a survivor."

You call your NGO a "Stop Wasting Food movement". Why is the word movement important in your cause and in the way you define your NGO?

"Because the Stop Wasting Food is not yours and not mine alone. It's ours. It's an all-inclusive movement where we all are part of the problem, and thus we are all part of the solution. Unlike other NGO's, we don't attack the industry or point fingers at the consumers. We are all in this together, we can all do our part to stop wasting food. That is why we are so successful. You see, Stop Wasting Food is not about what you can do wrong – it's about what you can do better."

I hear you, Selina, but the movement is in fact a pretty vague concept. Look at the political parties, who call themselves "movements" and yet they are still top-down controlled institutions with a base in the Senate. Wouldn't you say that Stop Wasting Food is also a top-down controlled institution, disguised as a movement?

"Well, Jonathan, Stop Wasting Food is definitely both a bottom-up and top-down controlled initiative. Every movement needs a strong leader, supporters and followers to power up the movement. But it also needs a clever board to steer the movement into a right direction and to keep moving. As above, so below – one cannot be without another. If you run alone, you might run fast – but if you run together, you will run far."

In our conversations, you have mentioned the word "empowerment". Quite a few times, actually. What is "empowerment" to you?

"Empowerment to me is to give people the tools to be in control of their own life. When you stop wasting food, you will start taking more responsibility for the world. You will start saving your time and saving your money. You will start respecting nature, resources and the people who produce the food. Suddenly, you are not just a usual consumer zombie. You are awake. You are in control. By one small, simple action: stop wasting food."

The word "entrepreneurship" dates back to the 13th century French verb "entreprendre", meaning "to do something". How do you correlate "doing something", power and entrepreneurship with a movement such as Stop Wasting Food?

"Neo from 'The Matrix' said: 'I don't believe in fate because I don't like the idea that I'm not in control of my life.' You see, you can either be a passive spectator of your life, or you can try to change it. I started Stop Wasting Food 10 years ago because I wanted to change something. Because I could no longer be a passive witness to the fact that while every 9th child, woman and man in this world are starving, we waste enough food to feed all the hungry people of this planet – 3 times over! So I took that frustration and turned it into power, and did something. And what I started 10 years ago is now inspiring millions of people all over the world. I don't believe in fate – I believe that each one of us is creating our own fate with choices and decisions that we make on a daily basis."

In many of your talks, you have encouraged consumers to use their power. But what's it all about?

"Once you realize that you are fully responsible for every one of your choices and decisions – and every consequence that follows your choices and decisions – you can take full control of your own life, and you will be able to restructure life into something much better.

Humans are indeed very powerful creatures and can create wonderful things, but many humans are afraid to use their power. Why? Because basically we buy things that we don't need with money that we don't have to impress people that we don't like. Once we let go, we will unleash our power. Life is indeed quite simple, but many humans are too caught up in their own drama to see the bigger picture."

As a social entrepreneur myself, I've always been wondering: how do you mobilize people? How do you make people believe in a cause as strong as you believe in? Can you give any advice for an entrepreneur on how to turn his/her brand or idea into a movement?

"You mobilize people if you give them purpose and make them realize that with small, simple personal actions, they can be in control of their own lives. I do it though Stop Wasting Food. Others do it though corporations, art, music or politics. But it all boils down to one thing: to empower people to change their lives in a positive way.

You start inspiring a small handful of people and you keep going and going and you never stop – and suddenly a small handful turns into thousands – and it becomes an escalating movement changing the world towards a better place. For me, it's been 10 years of focused work. And I'm only getting started."

JEFFREY HOLLENDER
A guide to social entrepreneurship

Jeffrey Hollender is a leading authority on corporate responsibility, sustainability and social equity. More than twenty years ago, he co-founded Seventh Generation and went on to build the fledgling company into a leading natural product brand known for its authenticity, transparency, and progressive business practices. Today, as a social entrepreneur, author, speaker, consultant and activist, Jeffrey's mission is to inspire and provoke business leaders to think differently about the role they and their companies play in society. Along the way, he's working to drive systemic change that makes it easier for businesses to become radically more sustainable, transparent and responsible.

First, 7 things to remind yourself every day:

1. Your passion: Only do what you're deeply passionate about. There will not only be bumps in the road, but trenches that look like they have no bottom. If you're not doing what you love, there will be too many opportunities to give up.

2. Your mission: Become the change you want to see in the world that your business will impact – and make sure you can measure your progress.

3. Your vision: Protect your vision by maintaining control. Money always comes with strings attached – make sure you know what they are.

4. Your partners: Find the partners and collaborators who know how to do all the things you don't know how to do.

5. Never give up.

6. Never give up!

7. Never give up!!

Next 10 Steps:

1. Business as a system of nature. Systems thinking is an essential framework based on the belief that the individual parts of anything can only be fully understood in the context of the relationships they have with other parts of the system of which they are a part.

2. Find and hire the right people. It's the best investment you can make. Always hire people who are smarter than you are. Make sure they are committed to the success of the business, and not participating for their own success.

3. Choose your investors with greater care than your friends: once you take their money, it's almost impossible to get rid of them – but they like to make sure they can get rid of you. At an absolute minimum, interview three other CEOs who have taken money from the potential investor. They should tell you what the experience has been like.

4. Radical transparency is the key to authenticity, and authenticity is the Holy Grail of good business. Be honest till it hurts. Be honest all the time. Share the good, the bad and the ugly.

5. Measuring what really matters. Measure what matters to your stakeholders, not just what matters to you. Make the measurements meaningful. Make measurements against predetermined goals.

6. Get out of your own way. Leadership is an art. Ask questions, don't always provide answers. Invest in your own growth. Stay humble and get humbler.

7. Ownership matters. Business must stem the dangerous concentration of wealth that emanates from a world of employees who have little or no stake in the companies for whom they work. Owners perform better than employees. Every employee should be an owner.

8. Corporate governance. Boring, but critical. Your by-laws should include sustainability standards, diversity commitments, how you will report on corporate responsibility, equity in compensation and what type of open dialogue you will have with your stakeholders.

9. There's no such thing as a free market. Make sure that you understand who has the deck stacked in their favor. At Seventh Generation, we sold tissue paper made from recycled fiber. The US government provides more than $1 billion annually to subsidize the virgin fiber industry making recycled fiber appear artificially expensive. For more details, check out the Friends of the Earth Green Scissors Report for a complete rundown of "bad" government subsidies.

10. Good vs. less bad. We've come to confuse "good" with less bad. Paper towels made with recycled, non-chlorine bleached fiber aren't good, they're less bad. So are organic vegetables grown in China and flown to the US, hybrid cars, even a bicycle if it's made with the wrong materials. There are "good" products, but they are few and far between. Locally grown, organic, grass-fed beef that builds up the soil and sequesters CO_2 qualifies. Buying used clothing at Goodwill, or taking a course at your local community college, as long as you get there on public transportation. Make sure that your enterprise introduces something good – not just less bad.

WHAT GOOD IS AN IDEA
IF IT REMAINS AN IDEA?
TRY. EXPERIMENT. ITERATE.
FAIL. TRY AGAIN.
CHANGE THE WORLD.

Simon Sinek

MICHAEL A. FREEMAN
Entrepreneurial minds on the edge of failure and success

Michael A. Freeman is a psychiatrist, psychologist, consultant and former CEO who serves on the faculty of the Department of Psychiatry at the University of California San Francisco School of Medicine. His clinical practice is focused on the treatment of people with mood, anxiety and attention disorders, and his consulting practice is focused on entrepreneurship and performance enhancement coaching. Dr. Freeman's research addresses the strengths, vulnerabilities, and mental health issues faced by entrepreneurs.

He has held CEO and C-level leadership positions in several public and private sector health care organizations.

Sharon is a charismatic clothing producer. She started a highly-profitable business with a novel business model in which mass production and mass distribution systems integrate proprietary machines, materials and management methods. She prototyped her system, attracted investors, inspired employees, launched her company and caught fire with customers. When orders flooded in, Sharon was euphoric as she and her team worked feverishly to grow operations and ship product. As her pace accelerated, Sharon became agitated. Eventually she stopped sleeping, had a manic episode and was hospitalized.

Chad and his cofounder started a digital marketplace to disrupt an old-economy business sector. While his friend engineered the technology, Chad was constantly busy with stakeholders and restlessly starting new projects without finishing old ones. He was easily distracted, he interrupted conversations by introducing great new ideas at inappropriate times, and he was frequently late. The company's high-profile launch hit a speed bump when Chad showed up at the right place on the wrong day.

Akira co-founded a global export company and was in charge of business development. However, he was unable to grow his Northern Hemisphere sales in Q4 and Q1. Determined to improve results, he invented an app that increased customer engagement and retention – even during his plummet periods. He then scored one huge sale after the next with impressive custom er retention and growth of sales within accounts. But when winter loomed again, he stopped onboarding new clients.

What do these three entrepreneurs have in common with titans of industry such as Andrew Carnegie and Ted Turner? They are successful paradigm shifters with a shot at greatness, who are both helped and harmed by mental health conditions.

How were these situations resolved? Sharon started mood stabilizers, made some lifestyle changes and learned to leverage the positive side of her hypomania while preventing the negative side from becoming a problem. Chad developed organizational skills, hired a detail-oriented executive assistant and learned to use ADHD meds. Akira shared his app internally and team sales skyrocketed. Since his slump was caused by Seasonal Affective Disorder, he was transferred to Equatorial markets where the sun always shines.

The DNA of entrepreneurship

What is the difference between entrepreneurs and the rest of us? Where do entrepreneurs get their motivation, creativity, social skills, ability to make decisions quickly, boldness, risk propensity, and their unique capacity to recognize opportunities?

Genetic researchers have tried to identify a DNA footprint associated with entrepreneurship – with mixed results. However, mental health researchers have found a distinctive set of innate personality traits that characterize successful entrepreneurs. Most mental health conditions are associated with distinct personality traits. The traits that drive success, and that are also associated with various mental health conditions, include:

Openness to new experiences and ideas: entrepreneurs try new things, consider different perspectives and enjoy being in unfamiliar contexts.

Achievement motivation and striving: entrepreneurs try harder and pursue ambitious goals.

Extraversion: entrepreneurs are energized by people, communicate easily and well, are good at socializing and networking and are interested in their social world.

Risk propensity: Entrepreneurs are bold and willing to take risks without being frightened or intimidated by the possibility of adverse outcomes.

Self-efficacy: Entrepreneurs have broad and diverse capabilities and rely on their own skills and resources.

Independence: Entrepreneurs don't fit into organizations well, unless they are leading them.

Proactivity: Entrepreneurs anticipate, seek opportunity and act rather than react.

Innovativeness: Entrepreneurs transform raw creativity into useful solutions.

Positive affect: Entrepreneurs tend to be optimistic, upbeat and enthusiastic.

While the personality traits that confer entrepreneurial success have been characterized, less is known about the temperament of entrepreneurs and the mental health conditions that are associated with entrepreneurial personality and temperament. Understanding this link is critical for entrepreneurs who want to stay balanced, and for the ecosystem of institutions that support entrepreneurship.

Understanding the mental health issues of entrepreneurs is made more difficult by the stigma and shame that is still associated with these conditions. Beyond stigma, entrepreneurs are reluctant to disclose their mental health issues because they fear this kind of disclosure will adversely impact the valuation or operation of their companies.

In spite of the challenges posed by stigma related to mental health conditions, our team of academic researchers and entrepreneurs set out to study the relationship between mental health issues and entrepreneurship. We evaluated the lifetime mental health profiles reported by 242 entrepreneurs, and a comparison group composed of 93 non-entrepreneur MBA students and faculty members from a university business school, and college undergraduates. To overcome the stigma problem, we set up an anonymous online survey.

This is the first study of its kind, and we are in the process of validating these results with a much larger sample of entrepreneurs and comparison professionals. In this preliminary study, entrepreneurs reported having:

- Significantly higher levels of depression (30% vs. 15% of controls)

- ADHD (29% vs. 5% of controls)

- excessive drug and alcohol use (12% vs. 4% of controls)

- and bipolar spectrum conditions (11% vs. 1% of controls).

Also, half of the entrepreneurs who reported having no mental health issues told us that their closest relatives, their parents and siblings, have genetically transmitted psychiatric conditions.

Preliminary evidence suggests that entrepreneurs have mental health profiles that are different from non-entrepreneurs. Are these mental health tendencies caused by launching businesses, or are people with these tendencies more likely to become entrepreneurs? Both are probably true to some extent. Mental health conditions are associated with the personality traits that drive success. For example, people with bipolar spectrum conditions tend to be extraverted, people with ADHD tend to be independent, and people with depression tend to have greater empathy that allows stronger connections with stakeholders. When people with mental health profiles embark upon the entrepreneurial journey, stressful events can trigger negative symptoms. For example, work demands that result in insufficient sleep can trigger mood swings. Complexity resulting from rapid growth can trigger overwhelm that leads to problems with time management and follow-through.

A user's guide to your entrepreneurial mind

Is it unusual for an entrepreneur to have mental health issues, or to come from a family with mental health problems? Preliminary data suggests that this is so common that it may actually be the norm.

What does this mean for future entrepreneurs? Our research suggests that, by learning how to outsmart the personality and behavioral propensities associated with innate mental health differences, entrepreneurs can deploy strategies to benefit from the strengths associated with their personalities and mental health conditions. For example, entrepreneurs who are extraverted can be particularly effective at adding value to their businesses through sales and business development. Entrepreneurs who are creative can be particularly effective at adding value to their businesses through product or process innovation and improvement. However these strengths can sometimes be "too much of a good thing." The extraverted business developer can inadvertently disclose competitive secrets. The creative innovator can introduce new product or service features that the market is not yet ready for.

So it is important for entrepreneurs also to manage the risks associated with mental health conditions that can lead to adverse consequences.

Sharon's manic tendencies allowed her to use her charisma to attract investors, employees and customers while she used her creativity and achievement motivation and striving to innovate, execute, and drive rapid growth. To prevent herself from going over the edge again, she learned how to regulate her sleep and use medications to prevent herself from escalating to the point of breaking down.

Chad's ADHD helped him recognize and exploit opportunities, build strong social capital through hyperactive networking, and solve problems creatively by engaging internal and external stakeholders. He learned new strategies and practices to improve his follow-through and strengthen his organizational and time management skills. He also redesigned his job in order to work closely with a detail-oriented administrative partner, and he began to use medications as needed to build on his strengths while limiting his vulnerabilities. For Akira, working in equatorial markets prevented his Seasonal Affective Disorder from interfering with his formidable business development talent.

Should people with mental health issues refrain from entrepreneurship because of their associated vulnerabilities? Or is it the other way around – should people with mental health differences pursue entrepreneurship because of the strengths associated with their personality traits? These are interesting and perhaps important questions, but they are irrelevant to most entrepreneurs who just want to start businesses and make things happen. Most entrepreneurs prefer entrepreneurship to any other kind of work, and would rather earn less and endure greater stress than be a cog in somebody else's wheel. The majority of new businesses fail, and the majority of entrepreneurs are already starting new businesses as their current businesses are winding down.

Given the intensity of the entrepreneurial spirit, the need for self-understanding and self-care take on a greater importance. The entrepreneurial journey is full of situations that can trigger the dark side of personality traits, and can exacerbate mental health symptoms. Fortunately, most of this can be managed well once it is properly understood. At best, mental health differences can power entrepreneurial success. Ideally, properly managed mental health differences need not interfere with great entrepreneurship.

INNOVATION

GUY KAWASAKI
Simple questions

Guy Kawasaki is the chief evangelist of Canva, an online graphic design tool. He is on the board of trustees of the Wikimedia Foundation and an executive fellow of the Haas School of Business (UC Berkeley). He is also the author of The Art of the Start 2.0, The Art of Social Media, Enchantment, and nine other books. Kawasaki has a BA from Stanford University and an MBA from UCLA as well as an honorary doctorate from Babson College.

There is a myth that successful companies begin with grandiose ambitions. The implication is that entrepreneurs should start with megalomaniac goals in order to succeed. To the contrary, my observation is that great companies began by wondering about simple things, and this leads to asking simple questions that beget companies:

Therefore, what? This question arises when you spot or predict a trend and wonder about its consequences. It works like this: "Everyone will have a smartphone with a camera and internet access." Therefore, what? "They will be able to take pictures and share them." Therefore, what? "We should create an app that lets people upload their photos, rate the photos of others, and post comments." And, voila, there's Instagram. (Inspired by The Art of Profitability by Adrian Slywotzsky)

Isn't this interesting? Intellectual curiosity and accidental discovery power this method. Ray Kroc was an appliance salesman who noticed that a small restaurant in the middle of no where ordered eight mixers. He visited the restaurant out of curiosity, and it impressed him with its success. He pitched the idea of similar restaurants to Dick and Mac McDonald, and the rest is history.

Is there a better way? Frustration with the current state of the art is the hallmark of this path. Ferdinand Porsche once said, "In the beginning I looked around and, not finding the automobile of my dreams, decided to build it myself." (From Forbes FYI, Winter 2003) Steve Wozniak built the Apple I because he believed there was a better way to access computers than having to work for the government, a university, or a large company.

Why doesn't our company do this? Frustration with your current employer is the catalyzing force in this case. You're familiar with the customers in a market and their needs. You tell your management that the company should create a product because customers need it, but management doesn't listen to you. Finally, you give up and do it yourself.

It's possible, so why don't we make it? Markets for big innovations are seldom proven in advance, so a what-the-hell attitude characterizes this path. For example, back in the 1970s a portable phone was incomprehensible to most people when Motorola invented it. At the time, phones were linked to places, not people. However, the Martin Cooper and the engineers at Motorola went ahead and made it, and the rest is history. Don't let anyone tell you that the "if we build it, they will come" theory doesn't work.

Where is the market leader weak? Three conditions make a market leader vulnerable: first, when the leader is committed to a way of doing business. For example, IBM distributed computers through resellers, so Dell could innovate by selling direct. Second, when the customers of the leader are dissatisfied. For example, the necessity to drive to Blockbuster stores to pick up and return videos opened the door for Netflix. Third, when the market leader is milking a cash cow and stops innovating. This is what made Microsoft Office susceptible to Google Docs.

"How can we make a boatload of money?" is not one of the questions. Call me idealistic, but the genesis of great companies is answering simple questions that change the world, not the desire to become rich.

DEREK SIVERS
It's all about the mindset

Originally a professional musician and circus clown, Derek Sivers created CD Baby in 1998. It became the largest seller of independent music online, with $100M in sales for 150,000 musicians. In 2008, Derek sold CD Baby for $22M, giving the proceeds to a charitable trust for music education.
He is a frequent speaker at the TED Conference, with over 5 million views of his talks. In 2011, he moved to Singapore and published a book which shot to #1 in all of its Amazon categories.
His new company is Wood Egg, publishing annual guides to 16 countries in Asia.

One of the most important concepts I've learned is the difference between the "fixed" mindset and the "growth" mindset.

It's a little bit like "nature vs. nurture":

People in a **fixed** mindset believe you either are or aren't good at something, based on your inherent nature, because it's just who you are.

People in a **growth** mindset believe anyone can be good at anything, because your abilities are entirely due to your actions.

This sounds simple, but it's surprisingly deep. **The fixed mindset is the most common and the most harmful,** so it's worth understanding and considering how it's affecting you.

For example:

In a fixed mindset, you believe "She's a natural born singer" or "I'm just no good at dancing."

In a growth mindset, you believe "Anyone can be good at anything. Skill comes only from practice."

The fixed mindset believes trouble is devastating. If you believe, "You're either naturally great or will never be great," then when you have any trouble, your mind thinks, "See? You'll never be great at this. Give up now."

The growth mindset believes trouble is just important feedback in the learning process.

Can you see how this subtle difference in mindset can change everything?

More examples:

In a **fixed** mindset, you want to hide your flaws so you're not judged or labeled a failure.

In a **growth** mindset, your flaws are just a TO-DO list of things to improve.

In a **fixed** mindset, you stick with what you know to keep up your confidence.

In a **growth** mindset, you keep up your confidence by always pushing into the unfamiliar, to make sure you're always learning.

In a **fixed** mindset, you look inside yourself to find your true passion and purpose, as if this is a hidden inherent thing.

In a **growth** mindset, you commit to mastering valuable skills regardless of mood, knowing passion and purpose come from doing great work, which comes from expertise and experience.

In a **fixed** mindset, failures define you.

In a **growth** mindset, failures are temporary setbacks.

In a **fixed** mindset, you believe if you're romantically compatible with someone, you should share all of each other's views, and everything should just come naturally.

In a **growth** mindset, you believe a lasting relationship comes from effort and working through inevitable differences.

In a **fixed** mindset, it's all about the outcome. If you fail, you think all effort was wasted.

In a **growth** mindset, it's all about the process, so the outcome hardly matters.

And yes, the mindset itself is not fixed. You can change your mindset just by thinking it through.

**IF YOU CAN'T
EXPLAIN IT SIMPLY,
YOU DON'T UNDERSTAND IT
WELL ENOUGH.**

Albert Einstein

TONY ULWICK
Customers buy products and services to get a job done

If you've heard about the jobs-to-be-done theory, you've probably also heard of Tony Ulwick. A pioneer within the field and the inventor of the Outcome-Driven Innovation (ODI) process.

Tony Ulwick is also the founder of the strategy and innovation firm Strategyn, and I (editor Jonathan Løw) had the chance to sit down and talk to Tony about his work with transforming innovation into a more systematic and predictable business process.

Most companies talk about the importance of knowing their customers, but in real life relatively few know their customers that well. Why is that?

Most companies are still very solution-oriented. When you study this dilemma, you discover that companies are very satisfied with their own ability to understand customer needs. They rate themselves as 'very or extremely satisfied' in 72% of the cases, so we don't really know that we have a problem.

One of the reasons we think we're okay at it, is that we get so much input on a daily basis and talk to thousands of customers and collect their input. However, this doesn't mean that we also have the right input, because despite of this huge number of customer interactions, we might know what we're actually looking for.

There is currently no agreement on what a customer need is, or what customer needs actually exist out there. This is where the jobs-to-be-done innovation theory begins.

What is this theory about?

It's a different way at looking at a market and defining customer needs. Instead of talking about solutions, you go to the customers and start discovering what kinds of jobs that they're trying to get done.

For example, one job that I'm trying to get done could be to listen to music and enjoy music. To get this job done, there are so many different solutions out there.

Before the development of modern technology, the job would be done by musicians. That was the only way you could listen to music. As time progressed, that obviously changed, but the job of listening to music has been the same for decades, well, for centuries.

So originally, the job to be done would be to listen to music. As I understand it, we have more complex jobs to be done today, such as: What do I want the music for? Do I need it for the next five minutes to relax, or do I need it for 3 hours for entertaining guests?

Yes. Depending on the answer, that is going to change the rest of the job.

Another element is the curation of the music. What music do I want to play? In which order do I want to listen to the music? Maybe I want the slow songs first and end up with the more elaborate songs. Finally I get to listen to the music. When I'm listening, I'm evaluating my experience. I might hear things that I really like and that I want to hear again, or maybe never listen to again. So I want to be able to modify, add, remove and delete.

This gives various jobs that need to get done, and this opens up for different kinds of customers segments and product solutions, but you have to start with the jobs that need to get done and really understand them and your customers segments more deeply.

Could you give another example than music to illustrate the idea of the jobs-to-be-done theory?

If you're a kettle maker it would be easy to conclude that people buy your product to "boil water" even though boiling water is just a step in the real job the customer is trying to get done – which is to "prepare a hot beverage for consumption". If you want to keep making kettles and do not want to focus on the entire job, then you are at risk of a competitor coming along with a solution that gets the entire job done on a single platform. It is not uncommon for a new competitor to overtake a market by finding the capabilities, resources, funding, technology and know-how to create an offering that gets the entire job done.

You describe different kinds of jobs that need to get done. How can a company decide where to focus?

It depends. If we go back to the example of music, one outcome, when you're collecting the songs, could be to minimize time. This means that the core job to get done is to organize all the songs in the desired order for listening. Another job could be minimizing the likelihood that the music becomes distorted at high volume.

All those statements are independent of any solution. We just talk about how people measure success to get the job done, and when you have these different outcomes, the progression of the process should be: Which needs are unmet? And after that: Are there segments of customers that have different unmet needs?

You call this desired outcomes?

Correct. Customers use a comprehensive list of metrics to evaluate success when getting a job done. These metrics, a special type of need statement, we call desired outcomes, and they form the basis for our innovation process – hence the name Outcome-Driven Innovation.

By knowing how customers measure value when getting a job done, companies are able to use those metrics to discover opportunities for getting a job done better and/or more cheaply, and to mitigate risk when defining new product and service offerings.

How do you gather the necessary data for this process?

We typically put together a survey from 500-1000 people and ask them a set of questions such as:

How important are the different unmet needs to you?

What solution are you currently using?

Given that you're using that solution, how satisfied are you with the solution?

All these data-points gives us the necessary foundation to figure out which needs are in fact unmet.

When we know this, we can start building a strategy. Again using the music example, perhaps 50% of the customers want to focus on the order of listening, whereas another 50% are happy with their current solution to that job, but have other unmet needs. We need to segment these customers based on their different unmet needs.

This segmentation is key to the innovation process that follows.

You have a 6-step model for your way of working with innovation. The theory behind this is the Jobs-To-Be-Done theory, and the practice is the Outcome-Driven Innovation. Correct?

Yes. Outcome-Driven Innovation (ODI) looks at every aspect of value creation, meaning every aspect of a company's growth and innovation, from the point of view of the customer. And it works for both improving existing products and creating new, breakthrough products.

It is based on one very important realization: Customers buy products and services to get a job done.

When you begin to look at innovation through a jobs-to-be-done lens, you first see that the goal of innovation is to create products and services that help your customers get their jobs done better. This is the way to create customer value and to grow your company.

Einstein said, "If I had an hour to solve a problem, I'd spend 55 minutes thinking about the problem and 5 minutes thinking about solutions." This is how Outcome-Driven Innovation works. The hard part is identifying and prioritizing unmet needs.

Getting a job done better means doing it faster, more predictably and with higher output. That criterion is universal across jobs and should guide research questions.

I've read that ODI has an 86 percent success rate – a five-fold improvement over the industry average. Why does it work so efficiently?

Outcome-Driven Innovation is a strategy and innovation process that ties customer-defined metrics to the "job-to-be-done", making innovation measurable and predictable. The process employs qualitative, quantitative, and market segmentation methods that reveal hidden opportunities for growth.

Looking through the jobs-to-be-done lens, we reinvented every aspect of the innovation process, including the way customers, markets and customer needs are defined; the way markets are segmented and sized and the way ideas are generated and tested. This is the secret behind the Outcome-Driven Innovation and helping companies deliver what customers want.

But what DO customers want?

What they want is products and services that get a job done better or more cheaply. Most people think and go to solutions. What solutions do they want?

That is the wrong way to approach it. Don't talk to them about the solutions. They only know what they see. They can't envision the microwave, if they're cooking on the stove. We really shouldn't expect our customers to tell us that. What they do want is to get a job done more cheaply, where they're experiencing trouble.

In this book we hear a lot about the Lean Startup approach. I know that you're not a great fan of this?

Correct. I think it's the reason why many startups fail. Their purpose is to fail fast and learn fast, but why?

They're constantly pivoting, because they don't have the answers. They just build something and take it to the customers, but what if they have picked the wrong customer segment? Then they have to do another iteration, go back and test again and so on. This process can go on forever, and it typically does, until the startup runs out of money.

The only reason to pivot is that you don't get it right the first time. The goal of ODI is to get it right the first time. It's hard and takes patience and insight, but our success rate is 86%, as you mentioned before. That is far greater than the 10% from new startups, and it all comes down to using the right kind of theory and practice when doing innovation and entrepreneurship.

So if you don't test using Lean Startup, how do you test and validate a product or solution?

We have discovered that customers use between 50 and 150 metrics (desired outcomes) to evaluate how well a product helps them get a job done. These metrics are the customers' needs. In addition, they use numerous other metrics to evaluate the execution of the related consumption chain jobs, which include acquiring, setting up, learning to use, interfacing with, maintaining, repairing and replacing the product. Traditional concept testing methods do not provide a qualitative means for capturing these metrics or a quantitative means for ascertaining their relative importance.

Our approach does both. Without these insights, accurate concept testing results cannot be achieved.

Well before concept testing, we use these same metrics to determine which customer needs are unmet and construct the solution that best addresses them. As a result, concept testing becomes a much simpler task because it requires only that we validate with customers that the proposed solution addresses the unmet needs (customer metrics) as well as we had envisioned. This is a test we are almost certain to pass because our concept has already been designed to be the product or service the customers want.

THIT JUUL MADSEN
Design-driven innovation

Thit Juul Madsen is CEO of the Danish design cluster
D2i – Design to innovate.

Works not just for LEGO - works also for smaller companies

LEGO had a turnover of DKK 35.8 billion in 2015 and more than 17,000 employees at the end of 2015. In all the markets where LEGO traded, it saw double-digit sales growth in 2015 (Trangbæk, 2016). This made the toy company one of the world's largest, together with Mattel and Hasbro. But it's not always been like that.

The story behind LEGO's turnaround in the middle of the 00s is known by many. The Billund-based company, which since its start in 1932 achieved unbroken growth until the end of the 90s, put its house in order from 2004 after a handful of gloomy years when the company was on the verge of bankruptcy. Shared Vision was the title of the seven-year plan to save the company. Employees were fired, there was a focus on earnings, and the risks of less remunerative business ventures were minimised by concentrating on the core business – designing, producing and selling toy building bricks (Robertson & Breen, 2013).

Back in the 1990s, before the business diverged from its course, LEGO was a sound Danish production company that made building bricks for children. Design was used primarily at the product level to form the bricks and building sets that could inspire children to use their imagination and play freely. One of the restoration plan's new aspects was that LEGO would now use design as a method for innovation and as a business driver, while involving their customers in developing new products (Feloni, 2014).

The number of special bricks was reduced and the focus was moved to standard bricks and building sets, which made the business more agile and able to react more quickly to market trends and changes in user behaviour and preferences. Once a robust base had been created, the time was right for development. User-involvement created a basis for designing products that to an even greater degree generated value for users and customers (Amarsy, 2015).

Much can be learned from LEGO. Design and design methods as tools for innovation are not reserved for businesses like LEGO. Small and medium-sized businesses (SMEs) can follow their example in a way that suits their situation and thus use design and design methods to reduce complexity, increase flexibility and innovate based on the needs of the users and a real understanding of the user context.

Design as a driver for innovation in SMEs

The debate about how the Danish business community is to manage in the future is to a high degree about a pricing race towards the bottom through broad cost-reduction exercises, optimisations and LEAN. But being aware of your costs is more a condition of existence than a competitive parameter. In order to differentiate in a constantly developing market it is a prerequisite that one has the ability to develop new products and solutions that are meaningful to the user.

And on that journey there is no way around the strategic use of design, which is what combines a deep understanding of context and user needs with product and business development. And reports in the most recent ten years have shown again and again that the companies that work with design philosophy and methods do better in international competition and are less affected by the changing state of the markets than the companies that don't. So let's take a look at how SMEs, even the less visible ones, can take a leaf out of the LEGO book.

Sausage rolls and hotdogs that are sold at motorway service stations are the core business of Easyfood. Traditional lay-by classics that we all buy once in a while, and convenience food is not a small market. Easyfood faced some challenges that in many ways were reminiscent of LEGO's. They had no innovation priorities, developed far too many products, and at the same time there was a large waste in production at a time when food waste was a burning issue. Just like LEGO, Easyfood used design methods to reduce complexity and increase earnings. They did this by dividing their products into groups named: basic, commodity and high-end, with appropriately varying requirements to assortment and pricing. This reduced waste and increased earnings. You can call that short-term innovation. They are also working with longer-term innovation, where the focus is on future scenarios. These scenarios are not just a forward projection of where the world is headed, but a description of a desired potential future – and how Easyfood can contribute to realising that future for their customers and thus also for themselves.

From sausage rolls and hotdogs to advanced electrical sockets

The Horsens-based company Neets produces AV control systems for conferences and education rooms and the like, and their challenge was the reverse of Easyfood's. They innovated too little, and when they did innovate it was rarely more than vague ideas on a paper napkin. Their innovation drowned in the day-to-day operations.

Neets started working with design-driven innovation a few years ago. Among other things, the business began by focusing on their users and on how their products were actually used – or not used. A deeper understanding of their users, their wishes and the challenges facing them gave a new basis for developing the company. Now their innovation is to a larger degree driven from the outside and in towards the company, rather than from inside out.

It sounds simple, but it is a difficult process when a business based on an image of itself as the expert that develops complicated solutions has to build a new culture in which the expert role is pensioned off and is replaced by the role of listener and observer who is sincerely occupied by the needs of the customers. For a business like Neets, this means going from primarily being interested in what an item can do and how well it does it compared with the earlier version, to also being interested in how ordinary people, who have difficulty in operating a copier, can use the company's advanced AV equipment without breaking into a cold sweat at an important meeting.

The result of Neets's changed approach to business development and their focus on the user and the contexts in which their solutions are used is clear – they are now present on most European markets and last year had a growth rate of about 20%.

Working with design-driven innovation is nothing new – everyone does it. Or, rather, many of the large, successful businesses do it, and many of the new market disrupters such as Airbnb, Netflix and Uber do it. But there is a giant undergrowth of less-visible companies that could release an innovation potential by introducing design methods as a tool for innovation. So these companies can also reduce the complexity in their business and increase flexibility. So they too can see and translate potentially important mega-trends into future expectations to their products and solutions. So they too can start to understand the real needs and wishes of their customers and users – and thereby contribute to realising desirable futures for their customers and users through the use of design.

Design-driven innovation is an approach to problem-solving and development with a focus on people and contexts, and it can be scaled to various types of businesses and challenges. Design-driven innovation is thus not reserved for guiding stars such as LEGO – smaller companies can also do it.

Here are five concrete pieces of advice if your business wants to use design as an innovation driver

- Ask someone who's done it – either businesses or design agencies.

- Be sincerely curious about your users – you may not know them as well as you think.

- Dare to drop the role of the expert.

- Invite designers in and let them give you their view of your business, users and costumers.

- Call me.

TORBEN WIESE
Appoint yourself head of innovation

Torben Wiese is an author who has written two best sellers, a public speaker and a teacher of breaking habits.

Have you heard that you must be "ready for change and innovative" – and thought "OH NO, not again!" It's your habits that are speaking. This is how you break your habits and reach your goals.

"The only thing that is constant is change," the Greek philosopher Heraclitus said over 2,500 year ago. Today that's truer than ever before – and at the same time change will never be as slow as it is today!

As an organisation, a leader, an employee and a private individual we can be vulnerable to change, but at the same time change makes it possible for us to reach higher, happier and better targets – more easily, more surely and more quickly – and is the best way of not falling behind but being a front-runner.

We typically deal with changes in one of three ways:

The organisation lets things slide – you do nothing and don't even see new opportunities/threats.

The organisation gets "assisted change" – new situations force us to act, but on the trailing edge.

The organisation carries out ongoing "voluntary" changes. All are leading-edge innovators, alert, open, humble about their own success and see change as an opportunity to retain what's good, achieve growth and targets, and as a means to avoid ending in undesired situations.

In a time of change, the voluntary changes create the surest and strongest competitive organisation, where you are change-makers rather than ready for change.

Are you also threatened?
No matter how much we are on the leading edge, and no matter how good (we

think) our products, services and prices are, there is already someone or something plotting to wipe us out and take our place.

That is something history shows us quite clearly in, e.g.:

- The energy sector, where things went from coal to oil, to shale gas and now green renewable energy.

- The auto industry, where makers of large, expensive gas-guzzlers are now going towards green and economical models.

- The hotel industry, where the largest previously had enormous investments tied up in buildings and overheads in the form of wages and salaries, where "the world's largest hotel chain" today is just an app that is run by a few innovative, visionary and creative people.

- The watch industry, where you can always see the time on your cell phone.

- The book industry, where only the best authors made it through the needle's eye and had their books published, while today everyone can publish, market and sell books via various websites.

- The grocery trade, where before 1,000 cars drove to the supermarket, while today one van can deliver groceries to the 1,000 people, who can now, simultaneously, use their time on something more interesting.

- TV and radio stations, where we previously had to accept their planning and tastes, while now, each of us can see what we want, where we want and when we want.

- The postal service, which previously lived on transporting letters, but which has now rediscovered itself and delivers parcels to us from our net shopping.

- The financial sector, where we used to go physically to the bank, while we now deal with most of our banking needs from home.

- The taxi industry, where previously we had to accept high prices and poor service, and where we can now be transported both more cheaply and friendlier in a car via an app.

- The music industry, where most music shops have now closed and we stream the music.

The question is: Are you on the list already; if not, when will you be?

– as we all will be, if we do not make a point of demanding innovative behaviour by all employees, each of whom must learn to think as a head of innovation.

See how things developed for others who didn't break their habits:

Nokia – the world's largest manufacturer of mobile phones missed the market for smartphones – Nokia's mobile business closed.

Kodak – the world's largest manufacturer of film in rolls with 12/24/36 frames had become resistant to change and believed they weren't on the list - Kodak's film business closed.

SAAB – the maker of one of the safest cars in the world was not able to adapt to the market and move from something resembling tanks to smaller, more economical cars – SAAB's car business closed.

Blockbuster – the world's largest retail renter of films didn't believe in online film, and now Netflix, HBO and others have taken over the market – Blockbuster has closed.

Who'll be next?

The brain loves habit because it:

- Saves energy

- Gives a feeling of security

The human brain was designed about 100,000 years ago, replacing the Neanderthals' brain (and they died out because they didn't adapt and develop!). Then – as now – the human brain was the smartest in brains, in what we could call version 1.0. However, our brains are still as they were then, but life has moved on and that makes completely different demands on our brains than what they were originally developed to handle.

Security is the most dominating psychological need – and the brain feels secure when we do what we usually do. Can you hear yourself or others say sentences such as:

- "Why change something that works?"

- "We haven't finished with the last changes!"

- "I am the way I am, and that's how they must accept me."

- "We're doing everything we can."

- "Actually, we have 20 years of experience in this."

- "We've tried that and it didn't work."

– then in brain terms it's all quite natural. Indeed, we often see organisations find a form of mutual security in a mutual insecurity about everything new!

The four archetypes of habit

Using a little caricature, let us consider four archetypes' ways of looking at and dealing with changes. Which type are you, and which type do you mainly have in your organisation – and what are the opportunities or consequences connected with this?

The Reactionary (Sees changes as malicious and is directly opposed to them – doesn't present new ideas).

The Sceptic (Is an onlooker, thinks statically and mostly – but not necessarily always – reacts in a non-cooperative way. May present new ideas, but mainly if they're to his own advantage).

The Constructive (Looks for opportunities in the new situation, exploits and implements the new situation. Presents ideas and proposals for change, also for the whole organisation – and is good at following them through).

The Developer (Sees changes as a necessity, makes them, thinks new – is innovative – has many irons in the fire but doesn't always take them out).

What brought you to where you are today will not take you where you want to be. One of the most important competitive parameters will therefore be your ability and motivation to think new and deal well with changes.

Your competitors also deliver good products and services, so customers buy where they feel an openness towards new things and with in those people who think of new things for the benefit of the customers and staff. We therefore wish to have the correct mix of leaders and employees in the organisation, probably a majority of Constructives and Developers. Never mind if the other types apply to work with our competitors – they probably won't anyway!

However, this doesn't mean that everything new is good and that we should mindlessly accept everything that's new and all new ideas. Having a healthy scepticism and saying "no" occasionally certainly also has its value. But no matter whether we mostly say "yes" or "no", we must always assess whether it has just become a pattern from habit, which then feels secure for us as employees or for the organisation, and if this pattern provides real security in a time of change, or whether it would be better to change it.

"Habits have deep roots" is a Chinese proverb, and it is true that it can be difficult to change something that feels good – and, as mentioned, everything that's "new" isn't necessarily good news. It is therefore important to have our targets, visions and dreams in view, so we fight together and hold on to the fact that we both can and should change and adapt. Or, as the old Indians said: If your horse is dead, get off it!

Congratulations. You are hereby appointed head of changes and innovations – large and small. It's them and you we need.

Habit-breaking greetings

Torben Wiese

WE DON'T SEE THINGS
AS THEY ARE,
WE SEE THINGS
AS WE ARE.

Anais Nin

DAVID COHEN
A small ask is better

David Cohen is the founder and Managing Partner of Techstars, the #1 ranked Internet startup accelerator in the world. Previously, David was a founder of several software and web technology companies. He was the founder and CTO of Pinpoint Technologies, which was acquired by ZOLL Medical Corporation (NASDAQ: ZOLL) in 1999. David is an active startup advocate, advisor, board member and technology adviser who comments on these topics on his blog at DavidGCohen.com.

I know many people. Because of this, I'm frequently asked for introductions by entrepreneurs that I meet. Usually they want me to introduce them to a person or company that is very well known and in large demand, that the person thinks can meaningfully help their business. Of course I want to help.

I always ask the targeted person if they want the introduction, vs. introducing them blindly. Most people say that they're happy to try to help a fellow entrepreneur.

Lately, I've noticed a very clear pattern. When I introduce two people, the person who wanted the introduction seems to always want to make big asks. Too many people start with "can we set up a 30 minute call?" Now, I know that many readers will say "Huh? That's a small ask." No, it's quite big for very busy people. Remember that time is often the most precious commodity.

A small ask is better. Remember that you're being introduced to someone who you know is getting this type of request all the time, but has offered to help. Just ask for one thing, and ask for it in the form of a response by email. If you have 3 questions, ask them by email instead of forcing the person to get on the phone with you real time.

I realize that you are hoping to build a relationship, which is why you want to jump on the phone with your newly introduced connection. But take it slow, make small asks, and build a relationship over time.

Here's how big an ask is for very busy people:

- Tiny = email response, 1 or 2 simple questions in a short email

- Small = email response, 3-5 questions in a longer email

- Medium = 15 minute phone call

- Large = 30 minute phone call

- Huge = In-person meeting.

Start small. Build to huge over time. I've seen this work very effectively, and I've seen large/huge asks quickly end potential relationships.

CÉSAR A. HIDALGO
To shape the economy, think like an author, not an owner

César A. Hidalgo leads the Macro Connections group at the MIT Media Lab and is also an Associate Professor of Media Arts and Sciences at MIT. Hidalgo's work focuses on understanding the evolution of information in natural, social and economic systems, and on the development of big data visualization engines that make available unwieldy volumes of data. Hidalgo's academic publications have been cited more than 5,000 times and his visualization engines have received more than 8 million visits. He is the author of Why Information Grows (Basic Books, 2015) and the co-author of The Atlas of Economic Complexity (MIT Press, 2014). He lives in Somerville, Massachusetts with his wife, Anna, and their daughter, Iris.

You might have never heard of Oswald The Lucky Rabbit, but in the late 1920's he was more famous than Mickey Mouse.

Oswald's story began when Walt Disney and Ubbe Iwerks – Disney's star graphic artist – moved to California. Disney and Iwerks had made a name for themselves in Kansas making animated shorts, but when the cartoons proved to be less profitable than they expected, they decided to move west. In Tinseltown, the duo gave birth to Oswald, who became the new darling of the silver screen.

But Disney and Iwerks did not own their creation. Universal Studios owned Oswald, and its executives used this ownership to extort Disney after Oswald became a success. The executives threatened to poach Disney's best animators if he did not cut down Oswald's production costs. Disney and Iwerks were deeply offended, but decided to avoid the legal battle – which they were likely to lose – and to focus on doing what authors do best. They created a new character in response to Oswald. That new character was Mickey Mouse.

Oswald's story teaches us that what is most valuable in an economy is not what authors make, but their ability to make it. The executives at Universal tried to extort Disney and Iwerks by holding one of their creations hostage. But this was a naïve move. While legally, Universal owned Oswald, technically they did not own the capacity to author characters like Oswald. That capacity was embodied in the minds of Disney and Iwerks, and this was the key factor that set the duo apart.

Understanding the perspectives of authors and owners is critical to understanding how authors and owners shape the economy. In the 1920s, it would have been easy to look at the success of Oswald and think that the character was where the value lay. But that interpretation, which is the owner's perspective, is grossly mistaken because the real value was not in Oswald, but in the knowledge, artistry and creativity embodied in Disney and Iwerks.

As further proof of that, consider Disney and Iwerks' next steps. After Mickey, they continued to push the boundaries of the film industry. Their next major project was a transcendental film: Snow White, the first full-length animated movie. At the time, the technology needed to create a full-length animated film was barely ready, and the project was considered ludicrous. Nonetheless, Disney invested all of his wealth into the project, and when he fell short, he borrowed money to complete the movie by showing an incomplete version of it to lenders. Disney was willing to lose it all again to achieve his vision.

But the story of Disney and Iwerks is not an isolated example of the economic superiority of authoring vis-à-vis owning. A similar story can be found in the story of Pixar, where Ed Catmull, John Lasseter and others pushed the vision of creating computer animated movies at great risk. Making a computer-animated movie in the early 1990's was as ludicrous as making a hand-drawn movie in the 1930s. But that ludicrousness did not stop Lasseter, who was unable to execute his vision at The Walt Disney Company and joined Ed Catmull in the startup that would later become Pixar. Together they triumphed with Toy Story, because among other things, they spent more than a decade developing the tools needed to author computer-animated films. Ironically, they suffered a similar fate than Disney and Iwerks, since The Walt Disney Company owned the rights to the characters in Toy Story. But once again, authors prevailed by punching back with new creations. In this case: Monsters Inc. and Finding Nemo. Ultimately, the Walt Disney Company had to accept the creative superiority of Pixar, and decided to join them instead of fighting them. Lasseter now heads the Walt Disney Company division of animation.

But why would anyone want to be an author, and go through the stress, grief, and heartache required to make something at great risk? Are authors simply driven by the expectation of a future payday? Or are they driven by something else? If you think that a future payday is what motivates an author, then you think like an owner. But the reality is more complicated that that.

Simple monetary rewards are not the primary driver of luminaries like Disney, Iwerks or Lasseter. Authors, more than owners, are looking to transcend, not because of ego, but because they want to contribute something useful, memorable, thought-provoking or inspired back into the world that inspired them.

So while Universal executives saw Oswald as a way to make cash, Disney saw cash as a way to make history. Disney was authoring the history of animation, just like Lasseter would decades later. Being the richest guy in the cemetery was not what their work was about.

Certainly, there is a role for owners in the economy. Owners can help scale businesses and manage companies during the long periods of decay that follow the creative thrusts that originate firms. But the wealth of the wealthiest owners, the wealth of Carlos Slim, Warren Buffet or George Soros, are pale accomplishments in comparison with the oeuvre of the greatest authors: The paintings of Picasso, the plays of Shakespeare, the induction laws of Faraday, the personal computer of Jobs and Wozniak, the cars of Ford and Benz, and the web of Tim Berners-Lee. For society, at least, it's authors who create value. After all, those who really shape economies are those who change what economies make.

WE DON'T KNOW WHO
DISCOVERED WATER,
BUT WE'RE CERTAIN
IT WASN'T A FISH.

John Culkin

MORTEN RONGAARD
The blockchain will completely disrupt your industry.
Are you ready?

Morten Rongaard is a Danish entrepreneur, CEO of Reality Gaming Group and the original brain behind the RealityClash augmented reality gaming app. Throughout his long and versatile career, he has worked on many different innovative project, taking on augmented reality and blockchain as his main fields of interest. He strongly believes in the potential of cryptocurrencies and innovation, and he is taking on different challenges to spread the word by being an ICO/crypto speaker.

I am completely Old Skool when it comes to games, and have been a hardcore Counter-Strike fan, since it was released in the year 2000. I still love luring my wife and kids out of the house to set up my old Amiga 500 and Commodore 64 consoles to play some of my favorite games, such as International Karate, Lotus Esprit, Crown of Ardania and Moonstone, just to mention a few.

But like all things in technology, things move fast. The Romans had a phrase for it – tempus fugit, which literally means time flies ... And time flies in technology like no other dimension.

Five years ago seems like yesterday, but in our digital world, five years feels like an eternity. What happened in 2013 feels like a century ago.

In those far-off days, I was mining bitcoin, which a good friend of mine – Jimmie Hansen Steinbeck – had introduced me to. I realised a revolution was coming, so I began reading up on the whole technology – especially the blockchain.

I was hooked from the first phrase I read: 'decentralized and secure'. The blockchain structure offers a peer-to-peer connection without any middlemen involved. Nobody likes a middleman.

Like buying beef from the farmer without the butcher or like buying whisky from the distillery without the off-license or bottle shop, this was direct business that I wanted to be a part of.

What I also loved about the blockchain was that it wasn't controlled by the government, the banks or any other management board.

Not only was it decentralized, the blockchain was also a digital ledger that could not be hacked. Every transaction was noted. Nothing could be retroactively changed, and it felt like pure and, most importantly, trustworthy technology.

So why is the blockchain technology so important? Let me try to explain that through the horse racing industry and humanity itself. Please bear with me. It will make sense at the end.

Take the UK horseracing industry. The whole core of this multi-billion market comes from just three Arabian horses that were introduced to the UK in the early 18th century.

In the following 400 years, these three horses have evolved into a huge amount of horses, some of which cost millions before they even run on a racecourse, but smart people still buy them.

The point here is that the people, including the British Queen, notable dynasties around the world and very rich men and women, completely trust the lineage and heritage of every horse because of their breeding. This breeding is another form of ledger and is a great example of a blockchain. Every 'family tree' of every horse is completely trusted, even if yearlings that cost millions turn out to be slow runners that never win anything.

So, if a blockchain of 400 years can be completely trusted by a respected billion-pound industry, what about another blockchain that is thousands of years old?

Yes, humanity. We ourselves are the ultimate blockchain. We trust our forebears are who they say they are. We believe in the family trees we are shown, and now, with DNA testing, we have further proof of where we came from. Our very bodies and brains come from a blockchain of our predecessors.

However, let's go back to the here and now in 2018 and the blockchain that came with Bitcoin and is now spreading across every industry. The word is so ubiquitous with the future of the internet that it's difficult to know what to believe.

The media has certainly helped to spread the word about cryptocurrencies, and after the tipping point at the end of 2017, every man and woman thinks that blockchain is just Bitcoin, and there isn't enough information about what blockchain technology is and what it does.

I hope that I have helped to broaden the picture of what blockchain is by the examples of racing and humanity that I've just given.

As I write this (15th of February 2018), the European Commission has just launched the EU Blockchain and Observatory with a fund of $300 million, to support research into the technology.

As the people in the EU know, blockchain doesn't have to be strictly related to cryptocurrencies, because blocks in blockchain can hold ANY type of data.

The blockchain came to notice, because it started with Bitcoin and cryptocurrencies, but what it does NEXT is going to completely change the world. It reminds me of the internet 25 years ago – if anybody can remember that far back.

Take the gaming industry, for instance. An industry that I love. While I am truly Old Skool in my gaming habits, it is the future of games that really excites me.

When blockchain-based solutions are applied to the gaming industry, they will be complete disruptors, and that's what I'm now focused on as an entrepreneur.

For the past five years I have been working on my geolocation-based first-person shooter game using augmented reality (AR) and blockchain technology with our own cryptocurrency called the Reality Clash Coin.

In the early stages of development, crypto and blockchain weren't even part of the idea. I had enough to do with GPS and AR technology, but over the last 24 months we did our research and have now integrated the blockchain into our game.

So why is there so little information about blockchain solutions, especially in the games sector? I believe it is because it's something new and the games industry doesn't like change … and we wanted to become one of the first to market.

For those who were into PC and console games, the invention of mobile gaming 15 years ago was not welcomed. To many, it was a useless new kid on the block and was initially derided. But then, as there is today, there were 'the true believers'.

It was only after the launch of the iPhone in 2007 and the breakout success of Angry Birds that mobile games finally reached their critical mass and were begrudgingly brought in the game fold. Some of those believers are now billionaires.

So as believers and huge fans of the blockchain, in August 2017 we launched our initial coin offering (ICO) based on the Ethereum cryptocurrency.

For those who are trying to understand the blockchain, try and see Bitcoin as gold. All it can do is act as an exchange for financial transactions. Ethereum (Ether) is more like a commodity such as oil or gas; you can do things with it; not just make payments.

One month after our ICO, we had raised 9,000 Ether as one of the first games companies in the world to have done so on this channel. I was thrilled to see that it wasn't just one big investor or a few whales, but more than 1,500 small backers supporting our vision and game idea.

Even though we are UK-based, two of the co-founders are Danish, so we consider ourselves as a partly Danish startup and the first in Denmark to have done an ICO.

Now that the funds were secured, we could finish what I had started five years ago, and my first talk to my team and co-founders was that we were going to disrupt the games industry.

We were new, we were one of the first, and this new technology was going to be the revolution I previously mentioned. We were going to lead the revolution.

My vision is for gamers to be able to truly own their character, their weapons and their resources. They should be able to trade, sell and buy securely using the blockchain.

That is instead of taking a risk on platforms such as Steam, where so many users have lost money and have spent thousands of dollars building up a profile they don't even own and have no control over.

I'm very happy with that type of disruption. Not just for the sake of it, but for making a real difference to gamers; the community I'm part of and hope I understand.

I want gamers to be able to sell their profile to others on a secure platform, if they want to, or even take their profile with them into a new game.

This is possible because with blockchain technology we can tokenize their profile and weapons because all of this is verified by being ERC20-tokenized, so, as owners, they are registered on the blockchain with a unique serial number.

Think about it like changing mobile operators, but keeping the same mobile number. That used to be very difficult, but now users only need to access their Porting Authorisation Code (PAC) from their old operator and they can move on. That's what you can do with your profile in our games.

People, and especially business owners, often ask me why they should spend time and resources on understanding the blockchain. My answer is simple, and I hope you will remember this advice:

Otherwise you will soon be competing with a blockchain version of your business, and it will be too late for you to compete.

Act now; time flies, make sure you fly with it. If not, like old technology, you and your company, games or otherwise, will be obsolete.

THE SILLY QUESTION IS THE FIRST INTIMATION OF SOME TOTALLY NEW DEVELOPMENT.

Alfred North Whitehead

NIRMALYA KUMAR
Invisible innovation

Nirmalya Kumar is Lee Kong Chian Professor of Marketing and Distinguished Academic Fellow at INSEAD Emerging Markets Institute.

He has written seven books, most recently Brand Breakout, and several articles in leading academic journals. These have attracted over 14,000 Google citations. As a consultant, he has worked with more than 50 Fortune 500 companies in 60 different countries.

He was included in Thinkers50 (the biannual listing of the top 50 management thinkers in the world), 50 Best B-school Professors (Poets&Quants) and 50 Most Influential Business School Professors (mbarankings.com).

New products such as the iPad or Facebook are visible to end consumers and the world at large. As a result, the companies and countries from which they emerge are seen as highly innovative. In contrast, there are a class of innovations that can be termed as "invisible innovation" because consumers do not observe them. Yet, they are just as transformative and they are coming out of India. Indian companies as well as R&D units of multinational companies (at last count 750 multinational companies including Astra Zeneca, Google, Intel, Microsoft, and Phillips had innovation or R&D centres in India) are leading this with process and management innovations.

Process innovations, or improvements in the way something is produced (in contrast with product innovations, which pertain to what is being produced), does not typically bestow the same global visibility on a company as does building something utterly new.

India may have an advantage in this kind of process innovation because of what Phanish Puranam and I call the injection of intelligence effect. The idea behind the concept is simple: companies in some of the less glamorous industries in India today employ people of a much higher calibre than do their counterparts in developed countries. Compared with the Indian workforce, Western employees with comparable qualifications and talent are much less likely to work on generics, metal forgings, call centres, or simple analytics jobs. The availability of talent at a reasonable cost often pushes Indian companies to assign, what the developed world would consider, overqualified people to relatively mundane processes. While it may demotivate some, this injection of intelligence can also lead to process innovations that provide the basis for globally competitive processes and products.

To take an example, perhaps only in India do millions of talented and ambitious young people aspire to work in a call centre! Once on the job, as would be expected, many of these people get quickly bored and start innovating. As a result, call centre companies based in India, like the Silicon Valley startup, 24/7 Customer, are changing the industry. The company developed tools that collated data about the past behaviour of customers and "mined" this information for patterns and other clues that might indicate their customers' intentions. 24/7 Customer's ServiceNext analytical tools can predict when customer service intervention is needed, and, if so, can then help formulate an individualized response. The technology is proprietary, and patents in the U.S. patent regime are pending. The underlying goal behind this innovative approach is to reduce redundant interactions and thus minimize call centre contacts, customer frustration, and, ultimately, costs.

This injection of intelligence effect can be observed in many other Indian companies, like Bharat Forge in the forging industry and DenouSource in the analytics industry, where "overqualified" people find ways to innovate in tasks the developed world has written off as "low end".

Management innovations, the implementation of a new management practice, process or structure that significantly alters the way in which the management work is performed, are typically invisible to end customers. Few make it into the spotlight of publicity unless their observers are enthused enough to write widely about them. Examples include GE's development of the modern corporate R&D lab, Du Pont's invention of capital budgeting tools, GM's adoption of the M-form organization structure and Toyota's success in harnessing the problem-solving skills of first-level employees. The Global Delivery Model, perhaps India's most invisible innovation, belongs in this category.

Invented – or perhaps simultaneously discovered – in the late 1990's by Indian IT companies, in essence the model allows the transformation of formerly tightly integrated work done out of one location in one company into a distributed format, where different parts of the work are executed in different geographies and by different organizations. The advantages that arise are obvious – to execute work where the best expertise for it exists, at the lowest possible costs; to take advantage of time zone differences for round-the-clock efforts; and to achieve some level of risk diversification if redundancy is built into the distributed model. The potential challenges are equally obvious – getting people to work effectively across barriers at the organizational, national, cultural and time-zone level.

Often critics ask, somewhat sceptically, about just how widely applicable the global delivery model really is. By now, everybody has probably heard the argument that goes "I still have to get my hair cut/eat my meals/have my tailoring and laundry done right here. Try offshoring that!" The usual rejoinder is "Fine, but I can book your appointment/reserve your table/do the actual stitching (as opposed to taking measurements) anywhere in the world". The point here is that given the attractions of wage arbitrage, people will find ways of decoupling systems of activities into pieces that must be done on-site and into others that can be done anywhere. The Global Delivery Model simply offers a systematic way to do this.

It seems intuitive that this may work for fairly routinized, mundane, standardized tasks like taking bookings. But can it work for high value added knowledge work – even creative work, like R&D or analytics? Actually it turns out, once you think carefully about it, that whether a piece of work can be executed remotely depends not at all on whether the work itself is simple and standardized. There are after all likely to be many, many more creative and talented people in India and China than in the US or UK, simply because of the much larger populations of both these countries, capable of doing highly creative non-standardized work, given the chance.

However, the possibility of remote delivery of a piece of work may indeed depend a great deal on whether its linkages to other pieces of work are standardized. If yes, then in principle, even highly unstructured, creative processes can be moved to remote locations.

In fact, we found something even more surprising. Even when the links between processes are not standardized, organizations are finding ways to be able to make them work together out of separate locations as if they were being executed in adjacent rooms!

Companies have figured out that engineers working in different locations are able to coordinate their iterative programming and bug-fixing activities, without need for extensive communication across locations. It turns out the engineers draw on their "common ground" knowledge that they shared and knew was shared, to be able to anticipate how others would respond to programming problems, and could coordinate their actions without the need for extensive face-to-face communication. This stock of shared knowledge came from their common training within the company, as well as through the use of workflow software that made the programming context of each site "visible" to other sites. To a naïve observer, sometimes the extent to which these engineers were able to coordinate their actions without the need for much direct communication looks almost like telepathy!

Implications of the process and management innovations out of India, especially, the global delivery model is leading both to lower costs for companies based in high-cost, developed nations, and to lower prices for consumers. Increasingly, Indian innovation has extended the model to more sophisticated tasks as leading firms are learning how to offshore more complex and creative tasks.

Western policy-makers need to realize that advances in the application of the global delivery model have transformed the traditional model. It has moved beyond jobs such as call centres and software development to more creative tasks as Indian firms find ways to divide and integrate even sophisticated work across locations. Advances in the model have overturned the traditional logic of moving people from the developing world to jobs in the West (immigration) to moving jobs to people through offshoring. These advances have also increased the contestability of not just low-skill service jobs but also high-skill innovation-oriented jobs, with resultant downward wage pressures in the West.

TODD HENRY
Being mindful of the rhythm of your life

Todd Henry is the author of The Accidental Creative, Die Empty, Louder Than Words, and Herding Tigers. His books have been translated into more than a dozen languages, and he is an international speaker and consultant on creativity, productivity, leadership and passion for work. Learn more at ToddHenry.com.

One thing we can all agree upon is that expectations in the workplace are only increasing, and that most of us are being tasked with doing more with less. Pressure is ramping up on all sides, and for those who work primarily with their minds, this means that we are being squeezed for more creativity on demand and to do things better and faster.

The problem, of course, is that you and I are not machines. Simply demanding efficiency doesn't ensure it, because at some point we reach a point of diminishing returns. In order to succeed as creative professionals in this "pressure cooker" environment, it's crucial that we take it upon ourselves to organize in such a way that we are prepared for those moments when we have to deliver results.

In my first book, The Accidental Creative, I outlined five core areas in which creative pros must be diligent and establish practices that lead to better and more engaged work. While there are no formulas for creativity or success, there are tendencies and patterns to be gleaned from the lives of the best and brightest that can help the rest of us emulate their success. The five core areas are as follows:

Focus
In order to succeed, you must clearly define the outcomes you are trying to achieve and allocate your finite resources against them. This sounds remarkably obvious, yet it's surprising to me how often I encounter organizations or individuals who haven't clearly answered the question "what are we really trying to do here?" Your mind is brilliant at solving problems and spotting patterns, but its scope of focus needs to be narrowed in order to be effective. Your attentional focus needs to be like a spotlight, not a floodlight. As a starting point, ensure that each of the projects or tasks you've been assigned has a clear

problem statement associated with it. This is the first step toward effectively focusing.

Relationships

The myth of the "lone creator" is a stubborn and dangerous one. While it's tempting to think that innovation is a solo sport, it typically results from groups of networked people running awkwardly after the same or parallel objectives. However, it's easy to become isolated in your work and fail to leverage the stimulation and beauty that comes from engaged, mindful relationships. To produce great work sustainably, you must be continually seek other people who (a) challenge your perspective, (b) help you see the world in new ways, and (c) open new avenues to resources and ideas. This won't happen by accident. As a starting point, identify a few people who inspire you and with whom you need to schedule regular times for conversation about life and work.

Energy

You can be the most efficient person in the world with your time, but if you lack the drive and energy to execute ideas when it matters most, you won't succeed. While many people think that the key to success is to squeeze ever more into their schedule, brilliant contributors recognize that the key to innovative thoughts is often to engage in addition through elimination. You must be willing to remove activities and projects from your life that are good, but not great. Great ideas happen most frequently in the "white space" of our lives, and when there is no room to breathe, we may lack the energy necessary to recognize them as they occur. As a starting point, ask yourself "what really good thing needs to go away so I can have the energy needed to focus on great opportunities?"

Stimuli

What goes into your mind ultimately comes back out in a new form. The stimuli you choose to surround yourself with will often determine the quality of your creative process, because they are the raw materials for your ideas. However, some of us are less than purposeful about the kinds of stimuli we allow into our process. We snack indiscriminately on videos, articles and whatever else is conveniently in our environment, but don't take time to fill our mind with inspiring, challenging stimuli that might take our process to a new level. As a starting point, set aside time a few times a week (or every day, if possible) to absorb inspiring and challenging books, articles or lectures. Take time to sharpen the amazing tool between your ears. If you want to have great ideas when you need them most, you must take care of your primary idea generation tool by giving it good fuel.

Hours

Time is the currency of productivity. At the end of the day, where you put your time in many cases determines success or failure. However, many people default to an efficiency mindset with their time rather than an effectiveness mindset. This means that they would rather squeeze in activity that gives them the immediate surge of accomplishment than work on activities that have little immediate return, but could pay dividends in the long run. As a starting point, consider how you might build activity into each day that is an investment in the future. This could mean developing a new skill, doing spec work, or creating something ancillary to your occupation but that fuels your creative spirit. Don't sacrifice effectiveness on the altar of efficiency.

Again, there are no absolute rules that will allow you to have brilliant ideas when you need them most, but the key is to recognize that brilliance at a moment's notice begins far upstream from the moment you need a brilliant idea. It begins with being mindful of the rhythm of your life, and ensuring that you are driving your work and not being driven along by it. Be purposeful, establish rhythm, and refuse to be treated like a machine.

CONFUSION IS A WORD
WE HAVE INVENTED FOR
AN ORDER THAT IS NOT
YET UNDERSTOOD.

Henry Miller

CHRISTIAN BASON
Without curiosity, innovation dies

Christian Bason is Chief Executive of the Danish Design Centre (DDC), which works to strengthen the value of design for business and society. Prior to joining DDC, Christian headed MindLab, a cross-governmental innovation lab, and the public organisation practice of Ramboll Management, a consultancy.

Christian is also a university lecturer, and has presented to and advised governments around the world. He is a regular columnist and the author of five books on leadership, innovation and design, including Design for Policy (Gower, 2014) and Leading Public Sector Innovation (Policy Press, 2010).

Christian holds an M.Sc. in political science from Aarhus University, executive education from Harvard Business School and the Wharton School, and is a doctoral fellow at Copenhagen Business School.

In most organizations, there is no shortage of barriers to innovation. But the most important – and the most commonly overlooked – condition for initiating and generating innovation is curiosity.

Curiosity killed the cat, claims the proverb. Excessive curiosity can put you in mortal danger. The more I have engaged in fostering innovation in business and public organizations, the more I have recognised that a lack of curiosity is at least equally dangerous. In fact, it can be so dangerous that it is often the explanation when innovation runs aground.

A story about the lack of curiosity

A few years ago, when I was head of MindLab, a cross-governmental innovation unit, we were about to launch an exciting innovation project together with a large municipality. The only problem was that one of the absolute key decision-makers in our partner organization was not of a mind to allow his organization's users or his own staff to be involved in the process. He may have had his reasons, but the organization's active involvement was an important premise for our contribution. My project manager had spent a fair amount of time in the municipality in question, endeavouring to explain the goals and methods. We had intense discussions about whether the project might still be viable. No one likes having to kill a project before it really gets off the ground. And it is fair to have concerns about where an innovation process might lead, if one's staff and users are going to be involved and engaged in new ways. However, at one point during our conversation my colleague hit the nail on the head: 'I think we could still pull this off, if not for his complete and utter lack of curiosity.' Right then I realised that we had no choice but to pull the plug on the project.

Decision-making: an exercise in optimisation?

The challenge for most large organizations – private as well as public – is that curiosity is stifled. The focus is on clear-cut and well-documented answers, strategies and decisions. The leader is expected to be virtually omniscient. This forms a paradigm and a mindset that is incredibly resistant to change, notwithstanding the turbulent, complex and dynamic reality we live in.

To understand the source of our widespread aversion to openness, curiosity and innovation, we might turn to the history books. Here we find the seeds of the classic organization and management DNA that we still carry with us today.

To find the explanation, we need to go back all the way to the founding fathers of management theory. First, consider Max Weber, the sociologist and originator of the idea of bureaucracy. He pointed out how specialisation and the functional breakdown of work tasks would help us build more efficient organizations. He underscored that we need to separate the person from the function if we want to eradicate corruption and unfairness. He demonstrated how important it is to make decisions on a neutral and objective basis. However, he also initiated a management tradition that has, to some extent, led us astray. Second, building on Weber's legacy, we have Herbert Simon, a Nobel laureate in economics and a founder of modern administration theory. Although, among other career achievements, Simon wrote an inspiring book on design, The Science of the Artificial, he never acknowledged the existence of such human traits as intuition or creativity. When executives make decisions, Simon said, they rely on analysis, experience and knowledge. What may appear in some managers as intuition or creativity is merely a reflection of their level of experience, which enables their rapid decision-making.

To Herbert Simon and his subsequent followers, decision-making is really about optimization. They were convinced that with sufficient knowledge and analysis, anyone would be able to reach the optimal decision. Decision-making was a science, an exercise in finding the right – optimal – answers. Roughly put, they approached organizational leadership as they would a mathematical equation.

From 'that's the way it is' to 'what if?'

This historical management DNA has stayed with us, handed down all the way from management theorists from the mid-20th century. Think about it: whether one is in an executive position in a private company or in state, regional or local government, it is not widely seen as legitimate to admit that there is something we do not know. Rarely can we motivate a new initiative simply by saying, 'we'll do this because we're curious,' or 'we'll do this although we don't know where it will take us.'

But curiosity is a crucial ingredient in organizational transformation. This has been known ever since the reputable organization researcher James March pointed out in 1991 that organizations need to balance exploitation (of resources) with exploration (of new possibilities).

Curiosity involves asking questions, such as 'How come ...?', 'How might we ...?' or 'What if ...?' Curiosity is not aimed exclusively at generating new insights. Curiosity looks to the future and thus acts as a key driver in the generation of new solutions.

Wanted: humility

I once had a meeting with a director in a public agency, who proudly proclaimed that he had now examined a new policy area in depth and felt confident in saying that he and his colleagues 'knew everything worth knowing' about the topic. I felt a chill run down my spine. How is that going to help anyone generate change in a complex, globalized society driven by new technologies, new behaviours and lifestyles and political turbulence? If decision-makers are so confident in their expert knowledge that they do not feel the need to know more, how can they formulate initiatives that are built to handle unanticipated circumstances? Even the most ambitious decision-makers in the world acknowledge that there are limits to knowledge and control. At least, they acknowledge it when they find themselves in the middle of a crisis. Not too long ago, I heard a leading German politician admit that no – no – government authorities had responded the way they should when the flow of refugees into his country was at its height. Perhaps the explanation is not that everyone acted incompetently, but that their approach did not incorporate a sufficient degree of humility in its failure to acknowledge that the world might change, and that one has to be ready to adapt when it does.

'What might be even more radical?'

Fortunately, there are bright spots. Some leaders are ready to embrace curiosity. In my own studies of the use of design methods among public-sector leaders,

I keep encountering statements revolving around curiosity. Take a public-sector leader in the welfare sector, for example a home care manager, who insists on asking the staff why they have a specific process when they enter the home of a senior citizen. The leader delves into details, asking why they say what they do, why this sequence of events, and how that affects the citizen's service experience. Or a school director who keeps asking, in a workshop on digital learning, 'What else could we do? What might be even more radical?'

Challenging assumptions

Even more fundamental is the inclination of leaders who are good at generating innovation in their organizations to continue to question their own assumptions. They are essentially curious about the accuracy of their own worldview. They are willing to create a space where their assumptions may be challenged – also by their own staff.

In the organization I am currently heading, the Danish Design Centre, we have deliberately devised a strategy where systematic experimentation forms the very basis of our work. That is not to say that we do not have a certain knowledge about what works, for example, when we match up designers and business leaders. But it means that we are always striving to remain aware that our premises and assumptions may prove inadequate. It is my hope that by being more humble in our role, we will ultimately be able to create more impact because we take a more open approach to the world. For the leader, this means relinquishing some degree of control to partners, allies and staff.

As one public-sector executive I know has said about the experience of letting the staff take charge of an innovation project: 'It meant a loss of control, but it is a positive loss of control.'

It it such a loss of control that the project partner whom my colleague and I once debated whether we could work with cannot tolerate.

MICHAEL MICHALKO
Change your thinking patterns

Michael Michalko is one of the most highly acclaimed creativity experts in the world and author of the best sellers Thinkertoys (A Handbook of Business Creativity), ThinkPak (A Brainstorming Card Deck), Cracking Creativity (The Secrets Of Creative Genius), and Creative Thinkering (Putting Your Imagination to Work).

Michael has provided keynote speeches, workshops and seminars on fostering creative thinking for clients who range from Fortune 500 corporations, such as DuPont, Kellogg's, General Electric, Kodak, Microsoft, Exxon, General Motors, Ford, USA, AT&T, Wal-Mart, Gillette, and Hallmark, to associations and governmental agencies.

Read the following paragraph.

I cdnuolt blveiee taht ppoele cluod aulaclty raed and uesdnatnrd tihs. The phaonmneal pweor of the hmuan mind. It deosn't mttaer in waht oredr the ltteers in a wrod are, the olny iprmoatnt tihng is taht the frist and lsat ltteer be in the rghit pclae. The rset can be a taotl mses and you can sitll raed it wouthit a porbelm. Tihs is besauae ocne we laren how to raed we bgien to aargnre the lteerts in our mnid to see waht we epxcet to see. The huamn mnid deos not raed ervey lteter by istlef, but preecsievs the wrod as a wlohe. We do tihs ucnsonius-coly wuithot tuhoght. Amzanig. I awlyas tghuhot slpeling was ipmorantt!

Amazing, isn't it? How are you able to see and understand a group of jumbled letters as words? How can you find meaning in a mass of jumbled letters? Show this paragraph to any child just learning to read and they will tell you that what you think are words is nonsense. This is because the word patterns in their brain have not yet become frozen. Our word patterns are so rigid that once we read the scrambled letters as words we no longer see them as a bunch of mixed up letters but as ordinary words.

The dominant factor in the way our minds work is the buildup of patterns that enable us to simplify and cope with a complex world. These patterns are based on our past experiences in life, education and work that have been successful in the past. We look at 6 x 6 and 36 appears automatically without conscious thought. We brush our teeth in the morning, get dressed, and drive to work without conscious thought because our thinking patterns enable us to perform routine tasks rapidly and accurately.

But this same patterning makes it hard for us to come up with new ideas and creative solutions to problems, especially when confronted with unusual data. In our paragraph, our word patterns are so hard wired that even a small bit of information (the first and last letter of a word) activates the entire word pattern.

Think of your mind as a dish of jelly which has settled so that its surface is perfectly flat. When information enters the mind, it self-organizes. It is like pouring warm water on the dish of jelly with a teaspoon. Imagine the warm water being poured on the jelly dish and then gently tipped so that it runs off. After many repetitions of this process, the surface of the jelly would be full of ruts, indentations and grooves.

New water (information) would start to automatically flow into the preformed grooves. After a while, it would take only a bit of information (water) to activate an entire channel. This is the pattern recognition and pattern completion process of the brain. Even if much of the information is out of the channel, the pattern will be activated. The mind automatically corrects and completes the information to select and activate a pattern.

This is why when we sit down and try to will new ideas or solutions, we tend to keep coming up with the same-old, same-old ideas. Information is flowing down the same ruts and grooves making the same-old connections, producing the same, old ideas over and over again.

Consider what happens when you read these words:

Thief............careless..........prison

Just three words activate a thinking pattern in your brain that relates a story about a thief who is careless, gets caught and ends up in prison. There is no story. There are only three unrelated words. Your brain simply recognized a certain pre-existing cognitive pattern and assumed the story.

The brain processes new information by immediately imposing meaning based on the dominant, associated, assumed context rather than objective inspection. Secondly, our judgments and decisions are often based on automatic, rule of thumb responses to this information rather than on thorough, logical analysis. The next sentence is a combination of letters and numbers. Note how your brain assumes it is a sentence by its appearance, and then responds by automatically identifying the numbers as letters they resemble.

S1M1L4RLY, Y0UR M1ND 15 R34D1NG 7H15 4U70M471C4LLY W17H0U7 3V3N 7H1NK1NG 4B0U7 17

It is this habitual use of pattern recognition that provides us with an instant interpretation of the problem. It also limits our view of the world, our access to new ideas and our access to unique solutions. If you always think the way you've always thought, you'll always get what you've always got.

An enlightening experiment was done by gestalt psychologists with a group of dogs: The dogs were trained to approach something when shown a white square and avoid it when shown a gray square. When the dogs learned this, the experimenters switched to using a gray square and a black square. The dogs immediately shifted to approaching the object in response to the gray square (which had previously triggered avoidance), and avoiding the object when shown the black square (which had not been conditioned to anything). Rather than perceive the gray as an absolute stimulus, the dogs were responding to the deeper essence of lighter versus darker as opposed to gray, white or black as being properties.

We have lost the sensitivity to deeper relationships, functions and patterns because we are educated to focus on the particulars of experience as opposed to the universals. We see them as independent parts of an objective reality. For example, if the average person were trained to approach something when shown a white square and avoid it when shown a gray square. When the squares are switched to gray and black, the human will still avoid the gray square. Once gray has been defined in our minds, we see the gray as independent and entirely self-contained. This means nothing can interact with it or exert an influence on it. It, in fact, becomes an absolute.

Over time we have cultivated an attitude which puts the major emphasis on separating human experience into different domains and universes. We've been tacitly taught that perception is the activity of dividing a complex scene into its separate parts, followed by the activity of attaching standard labels to the parts. For example, if the average person were asked to create a better zipper. The person would think in terms of pre-established categories such as "material zipper is made from, position of zipper on clothing, size of zipper, color and design of zipper, fasteners, zipper pulls to move the zipper up and down", and so on. This kind of thinking is exclusive. Its goal is to separate and exclude elements from thought based upon what exists now. It discourages creative thought.

You cannot will yourself to look at things in a different way, no matter how inspired you are to do so. No matter how hard or how long you think about a zipper, you will continue to see a zipper as an independent part of an independent reality and will continue to focus on the particulars of a zipper.

Change your thinking patterns

You can change your thinking patterns by focusing on the universal instead of the particular. When you do this, you will find yourself looking at the same thing as everyone else, but seeing something different. The essence of a zipper, for example, is fastening. Think of the process of fastening instead of the particular zipper. Now instead of thinking of the particular (zippers), open your mind and think of how things fasten (universal). Some examples:

- How does a wasp fasten to its hive?

- How does a window fasten to a sill?

- How does a bird fasten its nest to a branch?

- How does a person fasten a shoe to his foot?

- How do mountain climbers fasten themselves to the mountain?

- How do burdocks fasten to passersby?

George de Mestral, a Swiss inventor, occupied his mind with the idea of creating a better zipper. A creative thinker, he perceived the essence of a zipper to be "fastening". Thinking inclusively, he was always trying to connect all sorts of things with the essence of "fastening":

One day he took his dog for a nature hike. They both returned covered with burrs, the plant-like seed-sacs that cling to animal fur in order to travel to fertile new planting grounds. He made the "Aha" connection between burrs and zippers when he examined the small hooks that enabled the seed-bearing burr to cling so viciously to the tiny loops in the fabric of his pants. This inspired him to invent a two-sided fastener (two-sided like a zipper), one side with stiff hooks like the burrs and the other side with soft loops like the fabric of his pants. He called his invention "Velcro", which is itself a combination of the words velour and crochet.

The key feature of George de Mestral's thinking was his conceptual connection between patterns of a burr and patterns of a zipper. He bounced back and forth among ideas, guessing as to what works and what doesn't. By "guessing", what I mean is that he had to take chances as to which aspects of a "burr" pattern matter, and which do not. Perhaps shapes count, but not textures – or vice versa. Perhaps orientation counts, but not sizes – or vice versa. Perhaps curvature or its lack counts, and so on until he got it. The idea of Velcro is not only greater than the sum of its parts, but it is different from the sum of its parts.

Blueprint

Suppose you were challenged with the task of finding a better way to organize the way information flows on the internet. The average person will organize and think only about those particulars that relate to the internet, the way information is digitally organized, and the way existing search engines work.

What is the essence of the problem? How are things organized so they can flock and flow? The principle is "flocking and flowing".

Think about how things flock and flow in other worlds. Examples:

- How do fish flock and flow?

- How do molecules flock and flow in liquids?

- How do birds flock and flow while flying?

- How do sheep flock and flow in herds?

- How do people flock and flow in and out of football stadiums?

Xiaohui Cui at the Oak Ridge National Laboratory in Tennessee immersed himself in the problem of a better way to organize information on the internet. He did this by abstracting the principle of the problem (flocking and flowing) and immersed himself in searching in other domains for how things flock and flow. When he made the analogical connection between how birds of the same species flock and flow together and how information flocks and flows on the internet, he was able to look at his problem with a new perspective.

The system he created mimics the ways birds of the same species congregate while flying. He created flocks of virtual "birds". Each bird carries a document, which is assigned a string of numbers. Documents with a lot of similar words have number strings of the same length. A virtual bird will fly only with others of its own "species" or, in this case, documents with number strings of the same length. When a new article appears on the Internet, software scans it for words similar to those in existing articles and then files the document in an existing flock, or creates a new one.

Chi's new tool will, whenever you go online, automatically update your browser with any new stories added to your favorite websites. It will also provide automatic updates from other websites, such as when new scientific papers are added to journals.

Chi discovered the abstract connection that links and does not separate parts of two complex wholes by thinking of universals and essentials. He connected the flocking and flowing of information with the flocking and flowing of birds. This is the essence of creative thinking: a complex blending of elements of two or more dissimilar subjects, all of which involve guesswork rather than certainty.

SARA SCHØLER LASS
Innovation is not a show-off, but an impassioned and dedicated effort

Founder and owner of Zimplifi.

I am driven by new ideas, actions and trends within technology, digitalization and design. I love to create innovation, services and products that make sense to those who would use, buy and develop the solutions.

Behind my work is a solid experience as manager and leader within global companies in the B2B industry. My experience is focused around starting up and leading teams to be able to work with, develop and implement design and design thinking as a driver for customer experience, innovation, business and digitalization.

I have a Masters in Communication, Organisation and Strategy from Aalborg University, and International Management Education Programmes from IMD etc.

Often, I do presentations and talks for leadership teams about innovation, design thinking and customer experiences. One of the frequently asked questions from the audience, which in fact is also very foundational, is:

"How do you get started with innovation, and how do you ensure the focus on innovation is not just a show-off – but a part of a strong growth strategy?"

Innovation should not be the symbol of a boxing ball turning back and forth in the company, hoping it will sell some more tickets for the game by itself. It should be an intensive game to make the ball a central part of a growth strategy – aiming for new solutions and markets, involving customers and users, but also working and taking new and different decisions during the game, if and when this is needed.

The reason for my audience asking the question, and for me highlighting it, is that in some companies I experience that great business models, products or service ideas are identified, and a lot of ideas and opportunities are developed and ready to take off – but then something happens.

The takeoff does not become a reality, often due to excuses, such as the idea is too new, too different, it requires a new set-up throughout the value chain, it requires new competencies, and most of all risk taking. Or the ideas and new products are developed with an internal perspective, and not solving the user's need, but focus on technical features.

Innovation is not a success unless the ideas are brought to the market, generate growth and develop new markets.

Curiosity and asking the right questions to get started
So if you want to work with innovation as a part of your future business growth you need to consider the following steps to get started:

#1 An innovation effort needs to start with why
Simon Sinek is famous for his "starting with WHY", as a foundation for leadership. In this case it is also relevant for your innovation effort. Some of the questions you can ask to get started are:

- Why is it important for your company to work with innovation?

- What are your challenges: products, price, customer service, digitalization etc?

- What value do you want to create with your innovation, for your customers and your company?

When I do this exercise with my clients, I experience that by asking the above questions, a direction for their future innovation efforts and business opportunities begins. It helps to guide them on their way, but also to have the dialogue with their leadership team and employees about how far they want to go with their future efforts. Are they working with innovation mainly within their existing business, or are they creating innovation with new business models?

An example of a company working with the WHY is Amazon, where the vision is the following:

"The earth's most customer centric company. We want to build a place where people can come and find and discover anything they might want to buy online."

Amazon focuses both on the value they want to create, by being the most customer centric, but they are also clear on the main focus for products and solutions being within the online market. Furthermore, Amazon is a great example of a company that focuses on the traditional online market, but also experiments with new ways of delivering their products as new innovation.

#2 Stay curious - Know the trends and needs of your users and customers

Over time, most companies tend to forget to be curious about their customers' needs and problems. As they grow, they often get more focused on themselves and optimizing their product portfolio. It is a big mistake, as delivering great solutions and products starts with knowing which problems and needs your products are solving.

If you can answer what value your innovation creates for your customers, you can be clear on whether or not you live up to your purpose and direction with your innovation, and thereby better prioritize your efforts.

Knowing your existing and future customers is about being able to:

- Identify, who they are.

- Know what their problems and dreams are.

You need to identify: geography, age, gender, lifestyle, etc. And you need to know the number of customers you want to involve. It is important to consider how you want to get knowledge about their needs. Do you want to know more through searches on Google trends and data, visiting and observing them throughout the day, or making a quantitative questionnaire?

I recommend a combination. The personal contact with your customers gives you knowledge about their needs, and it creates a sense of loyalty and makes them brand ambassador, if they feel that you see them and perceive them in the right way.

An example from one of my clients is a situation, where I observed a user maintaining and using a digital system for controlling a boat. By observing instead of asking the user, we discovered that one of the biggest problems with the digital system was not the use of it, but the installation.

The system was so complex to install, and often the customers chose another supplier even though the daily use and design of the client's system was much easier. It made a change in focus for the client, so they started to reinvent the product to take both the use and installation into account for the future development, and added extra service business and contracts on top of it.

Combined with search on trends within digitalisation, consumer trends, and technology you can take the step towards your innovation.

#3 Involvement, try out, fail and redesign

Development and design of new products and solutions are not a linear process from A to B. It is a matter of going back and forth. As soon as you know and are able to structure the patterns of your customers' needs, you are also able to start the development of future concepts and products.

My experience is that involving your customers and users as early as possible in the creation and development of your future offerings, saves a lot of time and money in wasted products and concepts that do not match the need of the market.

Instead of inventing the final product, try to invite potential customers and users for a co-creation workshop or online campaign to develop future ideas.

It is also possible to make a concept drawing or prototype of the product and solution you want to develop together with a cross-organizational team.

It can be an app demo, a demo of a service concept or something else of importance for your innovation.

Go out, test it, get the feedback, and re-adjust your product and design so it creates value for your customers both in functionality, use and communication.

A lot of companies think it is difficult to involve customers in something that is not 100% final. Customers are humans, and they love to be involved, to be asked and feel important. Furthermore, it often benefits the value of the product, as you start to build up a loyal and engaged customer group that can help to promote the solution when it is ready to launch. Just be clear, the customer should not decide your direction, but be involved.

Another important effort is the internal perspective; create and involve a cross-organizational team. This is to ensure all perspectives from marketing, product development, sales, etc. are in focus. Also create internal commitment and engagement towards the future development and launch of the product. "Not invented here" is often one of the biggest obstacles for innovation, so make sure important role models and influencers are involved.

#4 Leadership, passion and direction

As soon as you have your future offerings in place, you need to make sure they make it to the market. It often requires courage, especially if you are dealing with a totally new offering. This challenges the existing business, as it might require new competencies within sales, product development, etc. In this phase, it is important that you ask the following questions:

- How does this product/solution fit our existing business?

- What does it require to get this product to the market?

- What competencies are needed to get it to the market?

Furthermore, you need to be aware of how you want to lead the innovation effort of your business in the future. This depends on the size of the company.

But you can start asking the following questions:

- How do you want to organize the focus on innovation?

- Is everybody measured on innovation, and should they be?

- Is your leadership and focus on innovation driven and measured by a desire for changing and developing your business rather than taking care of your own position?

The ability to create innovation is different from company to company, and there are a lot of elements that influence whether a company works with innovation as a show-off, or as a part of the growth strategy.

But a central part for every company is the leadership, the employees and the customers. So be honest with yourself, lead with passion, take risks, start involving and engaging the right people in the right way, to start your focus on innovation.

Employees and customers being dedicated to innovation are often worth a lot for a company because they are driven by passion, desire and the aim to solve needs and problems. They are rarely driven by a position. For this reason, they are willing to do, act and create value in a new way. So, give them focus, direction and decision power! Then they will work for your new business success, and you will see innovation happen step by step.

MICROSOFT IS ALWAYS TWO YEARS AWAY FROM FAILURE.

Bill Gates

NIKOLAJ STAGIS
Your business has the potential to change the world

Nikolaj Stagis is the CEO of the brand agency Stagis (stagis.com), which he founded when he was 20 years old. Now, 21 years later, he helps companies discover and develop business strategy and transform into purposeful brands.

Originally a graphic designer, the focus of his Masters from Copenhagen Business School, as well as a wide range of articles and a book, was on authentic organisational identity. Nikolaj is a member of the international think-tank Medinge Group who promotes brands as a force for good (medinge.org).

The brands I love are businesses with a meaningful purpose and a clear attitude towards who they are and what they stand for. The businesses are not necessarily charitable. They may not save lives. But they fascinate me and make me curious. I get the urge to try their services, work for them – become a part of what they stand for and the community that surrounds them. They are passionate about what they do and have their own special way of doing business.

The authentic companies have a meaningful purpose, use their history as inspiration to develop the future of their business, and are capable of passionately making their purpose come alive in the everyday. Some of the most famous companies are successful in redefining their unique identity in order to create connections between the organisation's strengths and the surrounding world, to which the business must be relevant. That these purpose-driven businesses succeed continuously in redefining and focusing their identity is because either the owners or the leaders are constantly curious about discovering and pointing out their company's special strengths. Look at Jørgen Vig Knudstorp at LEGO. Look at René Redzepi at Noma. Federico Minoli, when he rescued the Ducati motorcycle brand. Or Michael Christiansen in the period when he was head of the Royal Danish Theatre. No matter whether the starting point was taking over a company with a century-long history or starting a completely new venture, and no matter the services and size of the company, they were successful in developing their business in a way that was relevant and attractive to the company's customers and stakeholders. But they were only successful in their leadership mission once they made a virtue of understanding what the company's authentic strengths were.

Leaders must constantly develop the company's identity

To create a clear purpose, the company must be aware of the authentic strengths it builds on. A central definition of the term authenticity is being "true to yourself". That may sound simple enough. Many say that the company need only "walk the talk", which is the most widespread misinterpretation of authenticity. When thought and speech are implemented in the everyday "walk", it's about the company's integrity and ability to implement its beliefs in everyday life – not about authenticity.

When a company is authentic, it presupposes that it is true to itself – as opposed to e.g. following the customers, the market or the competitors. The primary challenge in being authentic lies in defining and understanding the company's "self". This should not only be understood as a specific permanent core of the identity – rather as an essential set of inherent strengths and potentials that are often composed of tangible and abstract characteristics, competencies, knowledge and ideas. Although such strengths have a certain stability and recognisability over time, they also change. Google's purpose is: "to make the world's information accessible", but there's a difference in expression between how Google made information accessible when the search engine was launched in 1998, and how the business uses information to develop self-driving cars and artificial intelligence today. However, Google's authentic strengths are to a large degree the same – then as now. Since René Redzepi and Claus Meyer first went on a journey of discovery in the geography, raw materials and food culture of the Nordic countries in 2003, the world's most influential restaurant, Noma, has redefined what "making local food" means. Today, René Redzepi is still exploring how "local food" can be interpreted in practice in the kitchen and the restaurant experience. This includes moving the restaurant temporarily to Japan and Australia to discover, interpret and challenge their local food cultures. Only now, more than ten years later, René Redzepi said that he was about to realise his dream of a Nordic restaurant when Noma reopened as an urban farm on the edge of the Christiania neighbourhood in Copenhagen (Denmark). When a company is true to itself, it doesn't entail a fixed meaning or permanent core to which the organisation must be faithful. Rather, the authentic companies are in a constant process where management and employees create new interpretations of the identity of the company.

There is a special managerial focus and a concrete leadership practice connected with achieving the dynamics that turn an organisation into an authentic company. In situations where managers successfully implement a turn-around and bring the business from crisis to success or create a new business that breaks with the market's usual ways of thinking, the managers are often driven by an extraordinary curiosity, an ability to go exploring and regard the business as if the manager was an anthropologist who had to understand an unfamiliar tribe. That's how Michael Christiansen described his greatest breakthrough at the Royal Theatre; it wasn't until he physically sat in the orchestra pit alongside the musicians and tried to understand them that he successfully rose to the occasion as head of not just the orchestra but the entire organisation.

Unlike "authentic leadership" or being an authentic leader, management of the company's authentic identity is about leading and developing the company while keeping in mind that there are unexploited potentials for development, innovation, customer experiences and better products hidden in the company's history, culture and employees – often unnoticed and invisible in the company's everyday life. This makes demands on the leader – middle manager, general manager or board chairman – to see opportunities in the company's praxis to the same high degree as seeing them in the company's figures.

Do you invest in future earnings – or in the future of us?

Apart from the banks, A.P. Møller – Mærsk is probably the company that Danes have mainly connected with big business and capitalism throughout history. If you ask Danes about the company's purpose, I think many will say "to make money". Mærsk's purpose or raison d'etre is first and foremost financial – at least in the Danes' view. That APM Terminals is currently investing DKK 14 billion in building a new port in Nigeria is primarily due to a belief that growth in Africa is long-lasting and that the terminal will become a good business in the future. The investment places A.P. Møller – Mærsk in a strategically important location and the venture draws a straight line back to the ability of the founder, Arnold Peter Møller, to see the opportunities of the maritime industry and generate long-term returns. But the port construction venture is also about the story of the Africans' access to cheap transport of goods, about new jobs – and thus about supporting the possibility for development for the world's poor. The good strategic investment thus contains a by-product of benefit to society, which surely pleases the leaders of the Mærsk group, but which is hardly their inducement to invest.

What would A.P. Møller – Mærsk achieve if the company changed its managerial focus from profitability to a broader perspective that balances the target of earnings with a target of creating a positive impact in the world? If the evaluation of a new project wasn't determined by financial yields but by the importance for the employees of the Mærsk group, for Denmark as a nation, or by the value that the project could generate for the world's poor, would the choice of investments then be different?

Corporate purpose isn't charity

At the world's leading enzyme company, Novozymes, new products that use enzymes for a wide range of industry uses are developed all the time. Enzymes can make detergents more effective, increase the shelf-life of bread and reduce the use of toxic chemicals in industry. When Novozymes was split off from Novo Nordisk and established as an independent company, the ambition was to create a viable business that would serve both society and the shareholders. According to its former CEO Steen Riisgaard, progress in the environment and sustainability are only possible if they are good business at the same time. Novozymes is therefore both: a company that makes the world greener and more sustainable, while at the same time it has been successful in achieving growth and yielding profits throughout the whole of its lifetime.

Novozymes's business model is in contrast to the way of thinking that is often presented when Corporate Social Responsibility (CSR) is being discussed. CSR is something that irks many business leaders as the company's responsibility is often formulated as a consideration beyond and additional to the company's operations and established purpose – and is therefore placed in an isolated department, remote from the company's core operations, strategy development and sales. That LEGO and Novozymes – and potentially also the Danish giant A.P. Møller – Mærsk – are successful in their social responsibility without talking about CSR all the time is because their purpose, core business and impression on the world are one and the same thing. When LEGO communicates its annual results to the press, the company also explains how children's brains and abilities develop when they play with LEGO bricks. Jørgen Vig Knudstorp and the LEGO management team have been successful because – said in popular terms – the company's financials and purpose are in harmony.

Identity is vital for the company's success

Authentic companies are often successful at being innovative, achieving a good financial position and creating value for society. They succeed in defining the organisational identity, purpose and business such that the brand is perceived as something special – by both employees, customers and the world around them. That LEGO is successful in constantly reporting a yield several times higher than that of its competitors such as Mattel and Hasbro, is due to both LEGO's success in asking a higher price and to its more efficient way of running its business. According to Jørgen Vig Knudstorp, LEGO has smaller staff and control functions than its competitors, while at the same time the organisation has a clear common focus, because the company's purpose and strengths are well defined. Both the value experienced by the customers and the efficiency increase when the company defines its purpose meaningfully.

Crises can lead to success

Unfortunately, few companies work constantly with defining their purpose, identity and brand as an integral part of their strategy and operations. They must often go through serious crises before the subject of identity and purpose arises – often in the form of questions like "What do we do now?", "What are we going to live from in the future?" or ultimately "Who are we?" Even though the questions often come a little too late, the crises also open up new opportunities. Some of the world's most successful brands have succeeded in taking a quantum leap in their development and strengthened their identity and brand after a crisis. When in 1982 the American medicine giant Johnson & Johnson was connected with seven deaths because someone had tinkered with the company's Tylenol pill bottles, the crisis resulted in an affirmation of the founders' attitude to give priority to doctors, nurses and patients rather than to the shareholders. As a consequence, Johnson & Johnson recalled 31 million pill bottles, offered to replace all the Tylenol pills on the market and developed a new three-level safety design for the pill bottles to ensure patient safety in the future. The crisis was thus a springboard for improving the product and strengthening the perception of the company's fundamental principles both internally and in the marketplace.

In 2015, Volkswagen was found to be involved in a comprehensive swindle with measurements of toxic NOx emissions from 11 million Volkswagen diesel-driven vehicles. The group's top executive, Martin Winterkorn, had to resign immediately, while the world press, the customers and the German government waited to see what the world's second-largest carmaker would do. Initially, Volkswagen put the focus on its coming electric cars and then went relatively silent, betraying the trust in the brand. As a consequence, the confidence in the brand and the Volkswagen stock price only recovered slowly. But if, in the long term, the company's new management was to successfully bring the VW brand back to its historic greatness, they would have to get to the front of the industry and show how swindle with toxic emissions could be avoided and how a trustworthy car manufacturer acts in today's world. Volkswagen's original purpose of creating a car for the people contains – as does the company name – an opportunity to develop after the crisis. How can VW become a car for the people to a greater extent than before? Through which products, services and communication will VW become not just "of the people" in perception but also in practical terms? If the new management exploits the critical situation and uses it in an age where social interaction, social (environmental) control, sharing economy and democracy take on new forms, and new global importance, it can lead to a new interpretation and a new meaningful life to the authentic company behind "the people's car".

JACQUELINE NOVOGRATZ
Values in tension

Jacqueline Novogratz is Founder and CEO of Acumen, a global social impact fund that has invested nearly $100M in 88 companies delivering agricultural inputs, education, energy, health care, housing and water to the poor in Africa, Latin America and South Asia. Jacqueline was featured on the cover of Forbes and named one of Foreign Policy's Top 100 Global Thinkers and The Daily Beast's 25 Smartest People of the Decade. She sits on the boards of the Aspen Institute and IDEO.org. Her best selling book The Blue Sweater: Bridging the Gap Between Rich and Poor chronicles her quest to understand global poverty and bring dignity to the poor.

All enduring institutions – and people – must hold contradictory thoughts to function effectively. At Acumen we recognize this need in the world and in our daily work. Indeed, our very values reflect those contradictions.

Rather than create a list of single words or short phrases that we see too often in corporate settings, we decided to create pairs of values that must live in opposition to one another. We wanted to say out loud what we know to be true: the work of creating change requires the moral imagination and, at times, courage, to consider trade-offs as we make the best decisions we can. To be effective, we need to know how to be both accountable and generous, when to listen and when to lead, how to be audacious while practicing humility. These opposing values all rest on the foundation of respect and integrity, two immutable values for the work we do, where the absence of either undermines our very purpose. We aim to be leaders who are not simply looking for a roadmap to follow, but are willing to challenge the status quo, to understand the world as it is, yet have the audacity and moral courage to build the world that could be.

This framework enables us to be more proactive and nuanced in designing and supporting the right solutions for a messy world where the poor especially have been left out of too many opportunities. For example, it is easy to agree that clean drinking water is a human right, but what kinds of delivery systems would ensure access to all while also insisting on efficiencies that allow us to use this scarce resource most effectively? What kinds of approaches are both scalable and sustainable? The same questions must be asked for healthcare, education, energy, agriculture, housing – indeed, all of the areas in which we work.

Even more specifically, how do we structure financial instruments that are generous and patient enough to enable entrepreneurs to experiment and fail, to discover what truly works for the poor, while also building in the needed accountability for success, both in terms of how the company operates and getting it market-ready to attract additional capital? How can we approach these challenges with the humility to admit the things we do not know while not allowing self-doubt to stand in the way of big dreams and aspirations?

Institutions navigating our interconnected, fast-changing world have a great opportunity to integrate such questions into their own strategies and decision-making. Indeed, a moral code for our shared future demands that we face squarely our responsibilities to one another while recognizing the need for competition, innovation, our very human desire to succeed, to be seen and, getting back to Brooks' column, to win.

I personally feel great optimism that we are embarking on a global path to more nuanced conversations. I see a growing number of corporations, non-profits, governments and startup companies asking themselves the hard questions about how to balance their short-term business issues with long-term institutional values, even when this does not yield easy answers.

Our challenge now is to design better systems altogether to merge the best of market forces with a much larger commitment to building the kind of society in which all of us have a chance to thrive, to win, and – always – to contribute. It isn't always comfortable, but changing the status quo never is. And in an increasingly complex world, that means finding ways to identify and balance values in tension as we work together to create the future we dare to dream.

HENRIETTE WEBER
Listening in the right places

Henriette Weber has been working on the internet throughout her career. She started out at Apple Computers and currently is Director of Brand and Involvement at the advisory group and digital studio Sustainia. For 12 years she has had her blog and company at henrietteweber.com and henrietteweber.dk where she has published ideas for business about digital development, branding, communication and PR. She is a consultant and board member in several Danish startups. She has been nominated for prizes as online pioneer as well as entrepreneurship.

Innovation has gone from 'somewhat inexplicable' to 'buzzword' to 'a must' for many businesses around the world. I think it is a way to address many of the demands for 'preparedness for change' from different stakeholders in the business that CEOs have to meet constantly. I cannot tell you how many times I've been hired by businesses to do something 'radically different' that ended up being exactly the same as what they used to do. Because they did not believe that if it was truly radical, it could be something for them. Because well ... it was different than what they are used to doing.

Being 'radically different' entails uncertainty. This is scary because you do not know if it will work. And what you are already doing – even if it's not working and you're losing money every month – at least you know how it will turn out. But deep down you know why it won't work: it's boring, inauthentic, and not a fit for you. In most cases it puts the business itself, rather than the users, audience, stakeholders and clients, as the center of the universe.

My business experience is not in thinking 'out of the box', which you could believe if you saw me speak at a conference. That perception of me is solid, maybe because I present in hand-drawn, comic-like slides. I still talk about corporate businesses, but in metaphors that people can relate to. 'Thinking outside the box' is nothing more than business jargon that does not say anything important. And outside the box is normally where things go wrong when it comes to innovation. Businesses cannot relate to it. Instead, I would suggest you make a very small box with your customers that you can put thoughts into – together. This makes everyone feel secure, inclusive and that they are part of the innovation process.

'Thinking outside the box' has always been a bit excluding for employees in businesses. In the vast majority of cases, employees see 'innovation' as something that comes from the outside, with a whole bunch of consultants who make visual drawings on tablets and research on computers. Everything must be effective, new and different, and much cheaper to meet the KPIs and define even more USPs. Everything is a little secretive to the employees of the business. Innovation should involve employees because it's they who will keep the innovation going when the consultants leave. It's they who are transforming bold ideas into everyday (exciting) worklife.

Why innovation?

Let's think about why we need to do things differently and innovatively. Is it a hunt for authenticity? We have come so far digitally now that the companies reaching the headlines of the business section and the case studies admired by the business world are not purely digital. They are a combination of digital and analogue. I would even say they are an analogue facilitated by the digital. They are listed in the old local phonebook; they have banner ads in football fields where local leagues are played; they set up booths at the local business center. The majority of their marketing budget is spent on the local. Not that much conversion on social media. No 'customer engagement'. Plain old 'word of mouth' (not the digital version) where you are referred to new customers because you did a great job on time, and you showed up at your customers' office every day, if needed. And this is not because an 'innovation consultant' told them that it's the way to meet their KPIs, or it's one of the USPs in their business. This is because it works for them. It has always worked in many industries. Take my godfather as an example: he runs a big carpenting business in my hometown Elsinore, Denmark, and have done it this way almost all the time. The carpenters there, who are spending a lot on ads and marketing, who are turning themselves into the face of their business, are seen as inauthentic and ostentatious: Maybe they need marketing because their work is not good enough on its own, or maybe they don't have good references?

I often share my godfather's story because he believes firmly that the best way for him to 'innovate' is to 'be authentic'. He simply shows up. He's visible in his jokes and his eccentricity – as well as his art and his craft that he has been building for a lifetime. He adheres to his principles and he gets more and more customers because he is just as he is.

The last thing he would invest in as a business? Social media. I think many businesses around the world would agree: You invest in social media because you start to see yourself as more of a media house than a business.

You want to be seen as somebody who is 'doing stuff' in your field.

The rest of us? We innovate out of fear of becoming the next Kodak or Block-buster.

For companies whose market suddenly disappeared,those which 'didn't see it coming' and ceased to exist, I wonder if they went out of business because they did not innovate. Perhaps they innovated in a different direction than the market? Perhaps they did not listen to what happened in the business world. Or perhaps they listened too much. I do not think it was a lack of innovation that drove Kodak and Blockbuster to extinction. Rather, they held on to something they believed in – a technology and business model they had used for years to grow, innovate and excel. But the market became smaller and smaller, and suddenly no longer existed. The market itself got eaten up by digital tools.

My best advice to people who want to innovate their business?

It is listening in the right places. And thus innovate in the right direction. To face the world with open eyes. To see what happens. One of the most import-ant questions you have to ask yourself today is what does your world look like after COP21 and the Paris Agreement? Are you going to be a part of the exponential growth of technology needed to tackle climate change? Busi-nesses cannot afford to ignore global challenges such as climate change, which will eventually affect them in one way or another. But if you listen carefully enough, you will discover hints that guide you in the right direction – one of which is the United Nations', 2030 Agenda for Sustainable Develop-ment, which outlines 17 Sustainable Development Goals as guiding princi-ples for all industries in all sectors across the globe.

And if you work with a business where the management does not believe that the world after COP21 will look different to them, then maybe it's manage-ment itself that requires a little 'innovation' and 'authenticity'.

YOU DON'T HAVE TO HOLD A POSITION IN ORDER TO BE A LEADER.

Henry Ford

MICHAEL E. GERBER
The astonishing spectacle of being stupid

Michael E. Gerber is a true legend of entrepreneurship. Inc. Magazine calls him "the World's #1 Small Business Guru" — the entrepreneurial and small business thought leader who has impacted the lives of millions of individuals and hundreds of thousands of companies worldwide for over 40 years.

Michael E. Gerber is the author of the mega-best seller "The E-Myth Revisited" and five other E-Myth books concerning small business and entrepreneurship. Today, Michael is on a new mission, to bring economic development strengths and capabilities to millions of people around the world by awakening the new entrepreneur within them. His one-of-a-kind entrepreneurial incubator called The Dreaming Room: Design, Build, Launch & Grow™, is now being led throughout the United States, Canada, the United Kingdom, Japan, Australia and New Zealand.

I thought it fitting when asked to include a chapter in an 'expert book', that I reveal to those who are in search of something or someone they seem to find absent in their life, that the 'expert' is predisposed to all of the vicissitudes of an ordinary life, and more.

At least this 'expert' is and has been.

It's a constant reminder to me, as troubles mount, blast away at me from seemingly every corner, and then, find resolution seemingly on their own, after a huge amount of trouble is created, of course, to just about everything and everyone surrounding me … it's a constant reminder to me that I know nothing, and seized by that nothingness, find myself walking or running down any number of paths that only have one thing in common, my blatant and resolute stupidity.

What do I mean by stupid?

Not the lack of information, necessarily. But the constant evidence that I have read just about everything I thought I knew, wrong.

My relationships, for example.

I fall in love so easily. Been married four times. Each of them was the love of my life. Each of them started out so innocently – if innocent can be thought of as youthful, naïve, blushing with embarrassment at being so unprepared for maturity. I'm still married to number four, thank God, couldn't even begin to imagine what would happen if I weren't. Not to her, she'd get along just fine, they always have; but to me. I'm the fumbling one, it seems. I no longer am out of one, but I'm in the very next one, as blithely as I got into the one before. That's what I mean when I say stupid. Everyone who knows me has cautioned me not too subtly – "Michael, remember ..." And of course, I don't. I can never remember, it seems. I can never remember the troubles, and how they started before. As far as I can tell, I'm incapable of remembering the troubles after they're gone. All I can remember, if it can be called memory, are the joyful, intensely good feelings I'm having in the present. Otherwise, I suppose, I wouldn't have been married four times. They each created their very own living hell. But, as soon as they're gone, it's gone. That's what I also mean when I say stupid.

But, it's not just stupid in relationships.

I seem to make the very same mistakes in business every single time.

No, they don't appear to be the same – in every case, they appeared to be much different. Each with its own flavor, its own form of originality. Its own form of brilliance. But, it takes me so long, so long, to figure it all out. I can be going on, caught up in the fever, or the pain, of a seemingly short term project, and find myself ten years later, still plugging away at it, looking for the diamond in the rough of my oftentimes, I'm sure of this at the time, sterile imagination. Plugged into an idea that never quite reveals itself, never quite speaks to me with the eloquence I'm looking for, never quite takes the form it has to take to become a living reality, never quite reveals itself to be exactly what I'm looking for, despite how many attempts I take at shaping it, refining it, discovering the raison d'etre of it, never quite nailing the necessary boards in place, to give it the posture it so badly needs, to stand up on its own, to say, "I'm here!"

And then, when it comes to me, it is so obvious.

Yes, I'm sure that's what they mean when they call me 'an expert'. That, once it comes to me, whatever the 'it' is, it is so obvious. So immediately obvious. So much so that it truly astonishes me that I hadn't seen it those many, many, many months before.

It's like you're in the middle of a paragraph, and looking for the exact words to say something which you just know is exact, yet it isn't there, it's hiding, if it's doing anything, it's not revealing itself, and I can't make it reveal itself, I can only muddle around in the middle of that paragraph feeling, oh so often, stupid, truly dumb, truly feeling like the idiot of all time, feeling like I could never write another word, another sensible sentence, another thought, by God, ever again.

Have you ever felt like that? Have you ever felt like you're a fraud? Have any of the other fellows writing their chapters here in the 'expert' book felt like a fraud, like they're pulling off the greatest heist of all time, but with little or no reward, even as they're doing it? That we're all, we expert, frauds, struggling from day to day, from paragraph to paragraph, writing anything just to hold on to our need to believe we actually know something, looking, if not for wise, at least clever, so nobody will catch on, that we're the most blazingly stupid men and women walking the face of the earth? Have you ever felt that way?

Well, take it from me, you're right.

If I were to list every single stupid mistake I've made in my life – I've actually attempted to do so in my books, but my publisher always warns me, threatens me, admonishes me, not to get carried away with it – it will ruin your reputation they say. Your readers will lose their fascination for you, they caution. Everyone makes mistakes, that's why they call them mistakes, they tell me. Yes, we know, you have the need to be candid, to be authentic, to be open and transparent. And it's an honorable thing to feel, they tell me. But, despite what's driving you to tell all, it's not only not an honorable thing to do, it's a stupid thing to do, they tell me. And so, I stem the urge, put it in the back of my soul, and save it for another day. Knowing, even as I do so, that I will rue the day I decided to shelve it, decided to keep it private, decided to only reveal my much applauded brilliance, and save stupid for another day.

But, you can only shelve it for so long.

My loving wife tells me that I need to shelve it too. Shelve this part of me which knows the truth. Shelve this part of me that doesn't seem to appreciate who I am. She tells me, constantly, as I fret and foam about how stupid I've been, and threateningly will choose to be in the near and not too far away future – what other disaster is coming my way!? – that I simply don't see the brilliance which surrounds me every day in every way. See? She says, as I bemoan the fact that I put on five pounds, seemingly overnight? See, you've written an entire new book over the past six months! And here you are fretting and moaning about five pounds! Let go of it, she says. No, you're not perfect, she says. Nobody is, she says, as she shows me her near to perfect figure in her near to perfect lovingly curvaceous skirt, which clings to her youthfully vibrant 20-year-old figure at 67 years of age!

And I cling to my next idea, my next breakthrough, my next challenge, my next new thing, my next 'expert'-inspired creation, with my 13-year-old mind, going as it is, on to 79!

WE DO NOT NEED MAGIC TO CHANGE THE WORLD, WE CARRY ALL THE POWER WE NEED INSIDE OURSELVES ALREADY: WE HAVE THE POWER TO IMAGINE BETTER.

J.K. Rowling

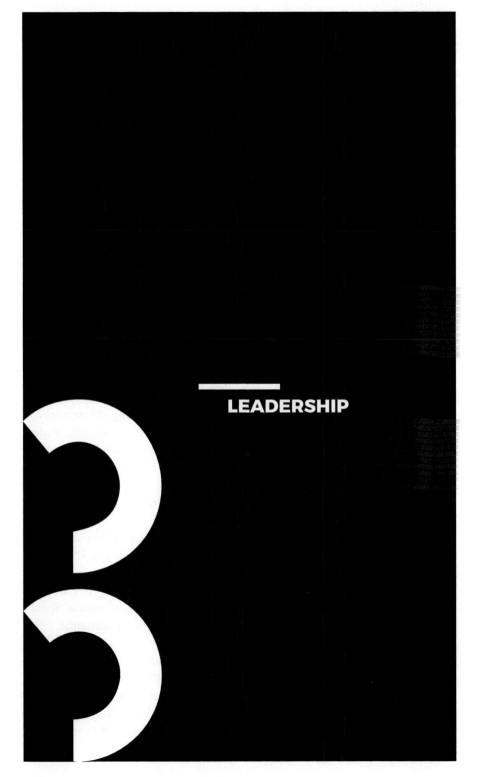

LEADERSHIP

ROBIN SHARMA
Authentic leadership

Robin Sharma is one of the world's premier thinkers on leadership in business and in life. He is the author of numerous books, including the #1 international best seller The Monk Who Sold His Ferrari; its best selling sequel, Leadership Wisdom from The Monk Who Sold His Ferrari; Family Wisdom from The Monk Who Sold His Ferrari; Who Will Cry When You Die?; The Saint, MegaLiving, and The Surfer, and The CEO. Sharma is also in constant demand across the globe as a keynote speaker for organizations dedicated to developing leaders at all levels and as an executive coach to people ready to create extraordinary work and personal lives. Clients include Fortune 500 companies such as Microsoft, General Motors, IBM, FedEx, Networks, as well as health-care firms and public sector organizations.

What would your life look like if you had absolutely no fear? What kinds of things would you do if you lived from a frame of reference that your thoughts literally could form your world? How brightly would your light shine if you stepped out of the limitations that are keeping you small and stretched yourself well past your comfort zone into the place that you know, deep within, you are meant to be? Authentic leadership is all about being the person you know in your heart you have always been destined to be. Authentic leadership does not come from your title or from the size of your paycheck. Instead, this form of leadership comes from your being and the person that you are.

Here are 10 things that authentic leaders do on a regular basis:

1. They speak their truth. In business today, we frequently 'swallow our truth'. We say things to please others and to look good in front of The Crowd. Authentic leaders are different. They consistently talk truth. They would never betray themselves by using words that are not aligned with who they are. This does not give anyone a license to say things that are hurtful to people. Speaking truth is simply about being clear, being honest and being authentic.

2. They lead from the heart. Business is about people. Leadership is about people. The best leaders wear their hearts on their sleeves and are not afraid to show their vulnerability. They genuinely care about other people and spend their days developing the people around them. They are like the sun: the sun gives away all it has to the plants and the trees. But in return, the plants and the trees always grow toward the sun.

3. They have rich moral fiber. Who you are speaks far more loudly than anything you could ever say. Strength of character is true power – and people can feel it a mile away. Authentic leaders work on their character. They walk their talk and are aligned with their core values. They are noble and good. And in doing so, people trust, respect and listen to them.

4. They are courageous. It takes a lot of courage to go against the crowd. It takes a lot of courage to be a visionary. It takes a lot of inner strength to do what you think is right even though it may not be easy. We live in a world where so many people walk the path of least resistance. Authentic leadership is all about taking the road less traveled and doing, not what is easy, but what is right.

5. They build teams and create communities. One of the primary things that people are looking for in their work experience is a sense of community. In the old days, we got our community from where we lived. We would have block parties and street picnics. In the new age of work, employees seek their sense of community and connection from the workplace. Authentic leaders create workplaces that foster human linkages and lasting friendships.

6. They deepen themselves. The job of the leader is to go deep. Authentic leaders know themselves intimately. They nurture a strong self-relationship. They know their weaknesses and play to their strengths. And they always spend a lot of time transcending their fears.

7. They are dreamers. Einstein said that, "Imagination is more important than knowledge." It is from our imaginations that great things are born. Authentic leaders dare to dream impossible dreams. They see what everyone else sees and then dream up new possibilities. They spend a lot of time with their eyes closed creating blueprints and fantasies that lead to better products, better services, better workplaces and deeper value. How often do you close your eyes and dream?

8. They care for themselves. Taking care of your physical dimension is a sign of self-respect. You can't do great things at work if you don't feel good. Authentic leaders eat well, exercise and care for the temples that are their bodies. They spend time in nature, drink plenty of water and get regular massages so that, physically, they are operating at planet-class levels of performance.

9. They commit to excellence rather than perfection. No human being is perfect. Every single one of us is a work in progress.

Authentic leaders commit themselves to excellence in everything that they do. They are constantly pushing the envelope and raising their standards. They do not seek perfection and have the wisdom to know the difference. What would your life look like if you raised your standards well beyond what anyone could ever imagine of you?

10. They leave a legacy. To live in the hearts of the people around you is to never die. Success is wonderful but significance is even better. You were made to contribute and to leave a mark on the people around you. In failing to live from this frame of reference, you betray yourself. Authentic leaders are constantly building their legacies by adding deep value to everyone that they deal with and leaving the world a better place in the process.

IF YOUR ACTIONS INSPIRE
OTHERS TO DREAM MORE,
LEARN MORE, DO MORE
AND BECOME MORE,
YOU ARE A LEADER.

John Quincy Adams

JOHN MATTONE
Three basic leadership types

John Mattone is a best selling author, the world's #1 authority on Intelligent Leadership and one of the world's most in-demand CEO coaches and leadership speakers. Recently, John was named as one of eight finalists for the prestigious 2017 Thinkers50 Leadership Award recognizing the world's top leadership authority and thinker. In 2013, John was awarded the coveted Master Corporate Executive Coach (MCEC) certification from the Association of Corporate Executive Coaches. He was then honored with the prestigious 2015 International Executive Coach Thought Leader of Distinction Award, in recognition of his thought leadership and his work as a global leadership coach. With the award, he received an honorary lifetime MCEC, becoming one of only four global executive coaches who currently hold this certification. In 2015, John Mattone's Intelligent Leadership was named one of the three Top Advanced Leadership Development Programs that Change Lives, along with programs by Tony Robbins and John Maxwell.

"Authenticity" is a word that is used all the time, but how often do we think about what it actually means? Generally, we take authenticity to mean the quality of being at one with oneself, and that's a good start.

On some basic level, "being oneself" is a given, because every time you make a choice or take an action, it is you who is doing it. But on another level, we can say that some of our thoughts, decisions and acts don't really express who we are. We've all occasionally said things we don't really mean, for example. Authenticity is bound up in philosophy, moral psychology, responsibility and identity.

The authentic leader is aware of his or strengths and limitations. He or she presents the real self to followers. An authentic leader doesn't act one way in public and completely differently behind closed doors. Furthermore, the authentic leader owns up to mistakes and realizes that "leadership" is a journey and not a destination.

Without character, you ultimately have nothing

The word "character" is derived from the Greek "kharakter", which means "engraved mark" or "imprint on the soul". In other words, character is a defining quality, but one over which each of us has significant control. Character may be "engraved" or "imprinted", but in the human sense it is "imprinted" on a living (and therefore changing) surface.

Your character is the sum total of the values etched on your soul, and whether you carefully "carve" your character or "hack away" at it randomly is up to you. In the end, however, your character will determine your value both as a leader and as a human being. The character you work at to define your soul, therefore, is an important determinant of your authenticity.

Inner core values; outer core behaviors

Your inner core as a leader, another determinant of authenticity, is made up of the self-concept, values, emotional make-up, and thinking patterns you bring to the task. Your outer core as a leader manifests in the leadership behaviors you exhibit. Better understanding of your inner core strengths and weaknesses helps you better understand how you come across as a leader due to your outer core behaviors.

Inner core values and outer core behaviors are part of every leadership style. Those who make the absolute most of their strengths and behaviors as a leader while still recognizing and understanding their weaknesses are generally the leaders that can be described as "authentic".

Three basic leadership types

I created the Mattone Leadership Enneagram Inventory (MLEI) nearly 20 years ago, and have revised, validated and tested it repeatedly since then. This measure of inner core maturity helps you understand what type leader you are, so you can understand your strengths and gifts that should be leveraged, as well as your weaknesses that should be acknowledged and addressed.

There is no one leadership type or subtype that is "better" than others, because each organization has its own leadership needs and requirements. But any leader who wants to excel must understand his or her inner- and outer-core strengths and weaknesses in order to be the most effective leader possible. There are three basic leadership types based on inner- and outer-core characteristics: those who lead from the head, the heart, or the gut.

Head

People who lead from the head have the gift of being able to think clearly and get things done. With sufficient maturity, these leaders can help teams reach new levels of achievement, but they must be aware of insecurities that can counteract their maturity as leaders. Head leaders can be divided into three subtypes: Thinkers (great problem solvers, who can nonetheless be indecisive); Disciples (who are loyal and dependent, but sometimes hesitant to act autonomously); and Activists (who have a positive outlook, but may use activism to distance themselves from pain).

Heart

The best leaders who lead from the heart understand the double-edged sword that is their emotions. Emotions are both their greatest strengths and greatest weaknesses. Those who lead maturely from the heart avoid selfishness, manipulation, jealousy and self-involvement. Subtypes of Heart leaders include Helpers (empathetic and great at handling conflict); Entertainers (who are charismatic and perfect when style and substance must stand out); and Artists (who are creative and innovative, but risk being too self-involved).

Gut

Gut leaders are strongly engaged with their world – a world from which they have high expectations. Mature gut leaders can reach agreements that others probably cannot, finding common ground as long as they avoid being too perfectionistic and paralyzing people with fear of mistakes. Gut leader subtypes include Drivers (who get things done, but can be overly assertive); Arbitrators (who identify common ground among divisive elements); and Perfectionists (who can get amazing results, but can be overly critical and potentially alienate team members).

Maturity level makes the difference

Knowing what type of leader you are is important, but it is your maturity level that makes the difference in whether you're an authentic leader or simply playing a role. Maturity means understanding your strengths and weaknesses, and knowing yourself and your leadership style well enough to know what situations, thought patterns and behaviors have the most power to improve or derail your maturity.

Thought patterns that accompany authentic leadership

Like leadership styles, people have predominant thought patterns. The authentic leader, regardless of inborn leadership talent, actively works on mastering various types of thinking as a way to actively work on leadership skills until they become automatic. Thinking patterns authentic leaders are aware of and committed to developing include critical, practical, inspirational, integrative, imaginative and intuitive thinking.

Critical thinking

Critical thinking is brain power. It's objectively sizing up a situation with efficiency by gathering information from reliable sources and then looking at the situation from more than one point of view. Critical thinking skills let you think a scenario all the way through and envision possible outcomes and implications that follow a course of action. Building critical thinking is lifelong.

Practical thinking

Practical thinking is taking information and goals and organizing them so that things are actually accomplished. Great ideas don't mean much if they're never put into action, and the practical thinker isn't afraid to do that. Translating ideas and concepts into real-world applications is the strength of the practical thinker, and the best practical thinkers are constantly innovating.

Inspirational thinking

Inspirational thinking is used by authentic leaders to inspire team members to be their best and reach their goals. It inspires "self-leadership" and depends on trust in team members' abilities and motivations. The inspirational leader can accomplish more than a leader who simply barks orders and expects them to be fulfilled. It's about bringing out the talents of all contributors.

Integrative thinking

Integrative thinkers see patterns and connections among abstractions and can create a coherent vision of a situation or a challenge. Integrative thinkers are hungry for learning across many subjects and understand that they are never "finished" learning. Integrative thinking is innovative, and is a thought style that sets exceptional leaders apart from the rest.

Imaginative thinking

The imaginative thinker is adept at creating something brand new from first principles. Leaders with predisposition to imaginative thinking can see possibilities and opportunities that might not be evident to others. When bolstered by strong critical and practical thinking on a team, the imaginative leader can innovate, disrupt and potentially change the game for everyone.

Intuitive thinking

The intuitive thinker has learned when to listen to his or her gut instinct. Intuitive thinking must be grounded by strong critical thinking skills, and when it is, the results can be astounding. An intuitive thinker who makes it a point to stay informed via history, data, and other facts knows when to make a counter-intuitive decision, and when it works, results can be amazing.

Conclusion

While the concept of authenticity could be distorted to mean remaining true to one's own demands regardless of the needs of others, this is ultimately self-defeating. Authenticity presupposes the demands of others and the "real world" and involves maintaining ties to collective "big questions" of worth that cause us to look beyond our own preferences. In fact, recognizing authenticity requires that we recognize others and their needs and points of view, whether those "others" are team members, customers or society at large.

Authenticity is what makes you "you", and it sometimes involves holding up to the light those parts of ourselves we would rather not recognize. The authentic leader isn't a completely different person in the copy room from the person leading the team in a project kickoff session. Authenticity is an integrated whole, an acceptance and development of the characteristics that are engraved in us. By cultivating authenticity, we not only stay true to our most deeply held values, but are able to get back on track when immature attitudes or actions derail us.

YOU HAVE ENEMIES? GOOD. THAT MEANS YOU'VE STOOD UP FOR SOMETHING, SOMETIME IN YOUR LIFE.

Winston Churchill

KEVIN KRUSE
And endless journey, never complete

Kevin Kruse is a New York Times best selling author, Forbes contributor and serial entrepreneur. His newest book is Employee Engagement 2.0. He can be reached at www.KevinKruse.com.

It continues to surprise me how many leaders attempt to be one way at work, while their "true" personality emerges outside of work. Once a CEO told me, "Leadership is acting." And yet he seemed shocked and confused when internal surveys showed that his employees don't trust him, they have low engagement and can't really wait to work elsewhere.

Authenticity has been explored throughout history, from Greek philosophers to the work of Shakespeare ("To thine own self be true." – Polonius, *Hamlet*). Authentic leadership has been explored sporadically as part of modern management science, and found its highest levels of acceptance with Bill George's book *Authentic Leadership*.

But what is authentic leadership? While different theorists have different slants on the concept, most agree on overall attributes …

Authentic leaders are self-aware and genuine
Authentic leaders are self-actualized individuals who are aware of their strengths, their limitations and their emotions. They also show their real selves to their followers. They do not act one way in private and another in public; they don't hide their mistakes or weaknesses out of fear of looking weak. They also realize that being self-actualized is an endless journey, never complete.

Authentic leaders are mission-driven and focused on results
Authentic leaders put the mission and the goals of the organization ahead of their own self-interest. They do the job in pursuit of results, not for their own power, money, ego or career advancement.

Authentic leaders lead with their heart, not just their minds

They are not afraid to show emotions, their vulnerability and to connect with their employees. This does not mean authentic leaders are "soft". In fact, communicating in a direct manner is critical to successful outcomes, but it's done with empathy; directness without empathy is cruel. And while emotional honesty is a powerful trustbuilder, authentic leaders also realize that emotions are contagious and irrational emotions are to be contained. As former Navy SEAL and TRX CEO Randy Hetrick told me, "a leader must learn to moderate and modulate the less-rational, more emotional fears that all humans face. If there is a significant, fact-based misgiving, then the leader needs to stop the train and address it. But if it is just one's own internal anxieties, the leader's job is to manage them and to project the confidence that a well-trained team deserves to rally around."

Authentic leaders focus on the long-term

A key tenet in Bill George's model is that company leaders are focused on long-term shareholder value, not just beating quarterly estimates. Just as George did as CEO of Medtronic and as Jeff Bezos has done for years at Amazon, leaders realize that to nurture individuals and to nurture a company requires hard work and patience, but the approach pays large dividends over time.

BASTIAN OVERGAARD
Less talk, more value

Bastian Overgaard is expert in silence.

Silence is frightening for many. Especially if it arises during a conversation. Then it's called awkward, embarrassing or deadly. And a lot of nonsense has been uttered over time with the sole purpose of drowning it out.

Yes, silence is noisy. The question is: What is it that makes the noise?

Silence is merciless towards what we're trying to repress. It sees through our ploy and tears our window-dressing to pieces. Nobody sees it as long as the music is playing. But if a so-called angel walks through the room, then we suddenly feel that we're naked.

As an authentic leader you accept your vulnerability. You know who you are and have nothing to hide. You will therefore stand strong in this raw, honest field, enabling you to use it as a hands-on management tool.

In 2003 I gave a talk about breaking habits. In order to take my own medicine and illustrate a point, I asked the audience to be silent with me for three minutes. When the time had gone I asked them what they had experienced. Several described the focus and intimacy that arose in the intense together-ness. No one found it embarrassing. We'd taken this "artistic break" together, just like when we show respect at a commemoration.

The audience's observations were acute, but there was a woman at the back of the hall who gave me an Aha experience and an important lesson in learning. She said: *In the silence I suddenly remembered that you're human.*

Together with several others in the hall, I grinned spontaneously at her funny remark. But a few seconds later it became clear to me what she meant. When someone steps on to the stage, we quickly put that person in a box. We lean back and listen to "the expert", and not the person, standing in front of us. He or she can be ever so wise, funny or motivating. There will still be a distance between us. Especially if the speaker isn't authentic and unconsciously hides behind his or her title.

That corresponds with the distance we know from the traditional hierarchy in a business. A management structure that is slowly becoming obsolete. Together with the leaders who insist on feeling superior to their employees.

During my talk, a few minutes of silence created a feeling of equality between me and the woman in the hall. After that experience I carried out a number of experiments in which I asked people to spend time together in silence. Both with people they knew, and complete strangers. The results were striking.

In the wordless room the participants experienced a high level of intimacy with and sympathy for each other – across their various career, age and educational backgrounds. My initial theory was that, since selfish agendas are often communicated orally, the ego is put at arm's length when we meet in arranged silence.

After I had explored this idea for 12 years and tested it in practice, I was confirmed in its potential. No matter whether I have facilitated silent networking events, silent dinners or silent walks, the experience of authenticity has been felt by all participants.

Another common thread has been the good and attentive discussions after the periods of silence. Silence, of course, cannot replace a means of expression as strong as the spoken word. It is more about creating a better balance between thinking and speaking.

Many businesses suffer from an unbalanced chat culture with self-promoting employees and leaders who've forgotten the proverb "Speech is silver, but silence is golden".

Innumerable meetings are held where everyone talks but no one listens. While one person makes his opinion known, another person is busy formulating his opinion. That is a direct abuse of the time spent at the meeting and is a particularly ineffective way of sharing knowledge. In comparison, I facilitate development workshops with up to 80% silence and 20% speech. And before these collaborations, most of my business customers believe they're taking a chance with a new, long-haired consultant and his weird concept. The very idea of silence projects images of standing in a circle and walking in the forest. But afterwards they tell me that they rarely have been as concrete, focused and efficient. The most incisive feedback came after a two-hour strategy workshop:

In the silence we can all have our say.

If you rest in silence you do not need to contribute to the verbal pollution. But there will always be employees who love to hear themselves talk. Don't count on them being able to stop themselves. Help them – and all the others – by facilitating obligatory artistic breaks. Even if it's only for a minute at the weekly meeting. Or a 15-minute silent walk. You'll discover that it doesn't only give you time to reflect and make better decisions. It will also create a more effective and authentic collaboration.

YOU CAN'T DEPEND
ON YOUR EYES
WHEN YOUR IMAGINATION
IS OUT OF FOCUS.

Mark Twain

LYNDA GRATTON
Eyes wide open

Lynda Gratton is Professor of Management Practice at London Business School, where she directs the program 'Human Resource Strategy in Transforming Companies' – considered the world's leading program on human resources. Lynda has written extensively about the interface between people and organizations. Her books cover the link between business and HR strategy (Living Strategy), the new ways of working (The Democratic Enterprise), the rise of complex collaboration (Hot Spots and Glow), the impact of a changing world on employment and work (The Shift) and the impact of longevity on society (The 100 Year Life – co-authored with Andrew Scott). In 2012 The Shift received the best book of the year in Japan and has been translated into more than 15 languages. She has been named by Thinkers-50 as one of the top 15 thinkers in the world.

If you're a business leader today, you are working to understand and balance the perspectives of an unprecedented variety of stakeholders – from NGOs becoming more voracious in their demands, to workers who are increasingly hard to engage – and doing so in a world that is more transparent and connected than ever before. It's a tough challenge.

I found myself reflecting on this the other night as I sat down with two very smart people for one of those marvelous European dinners. Both are business leaders in one of the world's great pharmaceutical companies. The conversation turned to the growing complexity of the business environment, and the question was inevitably posed: What had I, as a business professor, managed to figure out about what it takes to succeed under such conditions? In no particular order, here are my thoughts.

No illusions, eyes wide open

Some 15 years ago, my colleague Sumantra Ghoshal and I wrote business cases on three companies that were then leaders in their sectors: BP, Royal Bank of Scotland and Nokia. In one way or another, and for rather different reasons, all of these companies have since struggled. So my first observation is that leaders must constantly acknowledge that their companies are subject to an onslaught of destabilizing forces. Being vigilant and observant about the nature and velocity of these forces is crucial. Effective leaders in complex environments do not succumb to a belief in their invincibility – they keep their eyes wide open to the reality of the world.

Authenticity, tempered by custodial responsibility

Over the course of the dinner, we arrived at the hot topic of authenticity. Various proponents of this notion have urged leaders not to try to conform to a narrow description of what a leader does, much less copy someone else's style. Leaders are urged to be themselves. Only those perceived to be authentic and who are comfortable bringing their whole selves to work can gain others' trust and inspire them to pull together. It seems to me that this emphasis on authenticity is an important counterbalance to earlier assumptions that people gained leadership powers by dint of titles or positions in hierarchies. And it certainly resonates with the world's reverence for Steve Jobs, who created the world's number one brand while obstinately refusing to be anything but himself.

At the same time, growing complexity in the business environment creates a challenge. For people in organizations facing an external world of mounting chaos, being led by groups of highly idiosyncratic leaders, however authentic, could be confusing and distracting. In particular, when a leader is not a founder, he or she inherits a role as a custodian, and is entrusted with growing and passing on to future generations of employees and shareholders the value that past generations sowed. So yes, be authentic – but don't break the mold so completely that others need to spend energy figuring out how to engage with your leadership. The world is complex enough without this further variable to be considered.

Strength in diverse, collaborative teams

Thinking again about the problems encountered by BP, RBS and Nokia in the past decade, as different as they were, it's possible to see a common factor. These firms lacked diverse, highly collaborative leadership teams. At RBS, CEO Fred Goodwin isolated himself from his colleagues, failed to listen to others and became increasingly selfish in his behavior. At Nokia, the senior leadership team was for a long time extraordinarily homogenous (mostly men, mostly from Finland, mostly software engineers, mostly educated in Helsinki). How likely was it that they would be on top of the rapid developments in Asian consumer markets, or in technology and design emanating from Silicon Valley? At BP, we know top management found it difficult to integrate US assets and build collaborative relationships with the leaders of US acquisitions – contributing to a problem with implementing safety standards globally.

Simply put, as businesses are increasingly challenged by dynamic change and crises, it becomes ever more crucial for their leadership teams to have sufficient diversity to see what is happening from different perspectives, and sufficient collegiality to work collaboratively with each other even when under stress.

There is undoubtedly much more that could be said about leading well in complex business environments. Indeed, in a conference next month – the Global Drucker Forum, in the wonderful city of Vienna – I'll be participating in a bigger conversation. There will be more smart people seeking answers they can take back to their organizations. Together, we'll make the way forward for leadership a little clearer. And with luck, there will be time for coffee and strudel.

CHANGE WILL NOT COME
IF WE WAIT FOR SOME
OTHER PERSON OR SOME
OTHER TIME.
WE ARE THE ONES WE'VE
BEEN WAITING FOR.
WE ARE THE CHANGE
THAT WE SEEK.

Barack Obama

KARINA BOLDSEN
From "wannabe" man to a true power woman

Karina Boldsen is former HR Director at Vestas and currently works as Chief Commercial Officer at Solitwork.

It all started in a bank

My way of being an authentic leader essentially began in the banking sector. I had a superior who quickly noticed that when I got a task I was passionate about, I was unstoppable. (The same passion was in no way to be found in the work that I did not feel enthusiastic about).

One day he asked me: "What are you really passionate about, Karina?" He asked me to stay after work and think about what I wanted to be "world champion" at. He encouraged me to stay at the office that day until I had found out what I was really passionate about working with in the bank, and how I would pursue it. In the late hours of that dark night, I decided that I wanted to be the "world's best" at making the budgetary accounts profitable and create interesting approaches to expand the customer relationship with the bank. As the skillful leader he was, he could see that I created the most value when my passion was allowed to burn through, so I found my talent, and he let me engage in it.

It proved to be a crucial moment in my career, which made a difference to me back then, and which is still important for me now.

I took this experience with me when my career switched track and I went from developing money to developing people. By various routes and detours, "the bank lady" ended as Chief Commercial Officer at Solitwork, and although the road between them was long, there has always been a common denominator: I have let my passion create value and have been allowed to fulfill untapped potential. After the key turning point, I discovered the importance of authenticity. You must listen to your passion and pursue it – and that I have subsequently used as a beacon in my career.

The driving force behind my work

My favorite quote is "Do everything with passion – or not at all". But what is my passion? It is to get untapped potential unleashed. Potential in people, projects as well as companies: If there is untapped potential, it drives me to unleash it. That is why I invest my time in board as well as talent work, where I get the opportunity to bring out potential and make it productive. At one and the same time, it also sharpens my own management skills, since I am trying to keep the passion and inspiration thriving. I also do a lot of running in my spare time and have been participating in a number of marathons. This brings out the willpower in me, which I try to channel into my work by being a strong role model for my employees.

This investment in my passion played a key role in my decision to start my own company, Karina+, in 2013. At Karina+ I am the companies' "trusted adviser", and my mission is to meet the value-creating potential. It can, however, only be done as an advisor or leader if one brings passion and authenticity into it. But why do I really believe that authenticity and passion are the most relevant in a book about leadership?

Targeted work with passion gives impassioned solutions. Solutions that are created by enthusiasts, and who invest their time, their knowledge and their strengths – and a little piece of themselves in order to achieve the ultimate solutions. When all this merges into a higher unity, the desire to be a significant part of the company is created, and you will want to recommend it to others. That is value adding from both an employer branding and sales perspective, since authentic leadership creates passionate employees who will be good ambassadors for the company. The unfolding of the passion therefore already starts in the recruitment phase, where we must be enormously selective – and very skilled. However, it is not enough to be good at what you do, you must also be capable of being successful.

Authentic leadership is value-creating management

If passion is a great part of value-creating management, then authenticity is the frame. Authenticity is first and foremost about receptiveness and courage. Receptiveness to one's employees that rests on the recognition that you as manager cannot know everything. Therefore, one must listen, trust and then delegate. Courage is to a large extent about bringing skills into play in non-traditional contexts. Thus, as leader, you give room for innovation. But ultimately, the authenticity must come from the leader.

As leaders, we can easily trammel the employees' passion if we do not dare to delegate and let innovative powers become effective. It requires choices.

Opt-out, options and courage. Especially courage is essential in authentic leadership, where you as the leader must have the courage to let staff grow and follow their passion, as my former boss at the bank had the courage to do. But authentic leadership also applies to the leader. Courage must similarly be there to be authentic as a leader and you must be yourself.

After I stopped working at Vestas, I forced myself to reconsider myself as leader: my image, my field, my appearance, yes, in short: EVERYTHING. Was there a balance? Was I authentic? After a quick count, I had to admit that my wardrobe consisted of 12 black suits and 18 white cuff shirts. I was a "wannabe" man on the outside, but inside I felt more like a power woman. Therefore, I decided to be true to myself and strive for authenticity – something that I also think benefited my leadership skills. It is not a style guide, but rather a call to be true to yourself. It will surely rub off on your leadership and thus your employees. And as Oscar Wilde said: "Be yourself, everyone else is taken."

As manager, you can always be better. Smarter, more capable and more authentic. I strive at always getting better at what I do, among other things, by working with talents.

Be Inspired by talents – It is never too late to learn

I have been working with talent development for the past 20 years. Not only because it is important for innovation and growth, but also because it is crucial for me and my management style. Talent work keeps me sharp on the latest knowledge, while I constantly become inspired to challenge myself and go other ways – but I also keep some some "old-school" principles.

The realization that it is never too late to learn is for me one of the cornerstones of authentic leadership. The best leaders are those who continue to develop and improve themselves. Therefore, I have had interns from the University of Aarhus since 1998, which can be both demanding and challenging, but always rewarding in the end. Also through my board work at Studenterhus Aarhus, Aarhus Business College and Akademiet for Talentfulde Unge, I am inspired by talents. But I am also forced to think differently, because I am confronted with new ideas, new methods and new ways of seeing things. I am allowed to pass on my experience and get new knowledge in return. The talent work helps to boost my passion and strengthen my leadership.

In my career, I have learned that good leaders must be themselves, listen to their passion and be inspired by talents – that is authentic leadership, and that creates value!

WE ARE WHAT WE
REPEATEDLY DO.
EXCELLENCE, THEN,
IS NOT AN ACT,
BUT A HABIT.

Aristotle

PETER KREINER
How you create a global success - and an experience that lasts

Peter Kreiner is the managing director of the world-famous restaurant Noma and is responsible for a number of areas, including business development and administration.

Since I started at Noma eight years ago, my desk has been located close to the kitchen. That has led me to be aware the whole time of the key to this restaurant: 80 employees who are wholly and utterly dedicated to making people happy. In an increasingly digital and impersonal world, they work with their hands, are constantly in motion and are smiling.

It's been obvious from the start of my time here that the typical PR strategy would never work for us. Instead – and this may sound a little banal – we focus our resources on treating those who eat here as guests and not as customers. Noma is probably known around the world for pushing at the limits and discovering new tastes, but at its core the restaurant was founded in a timeless sense of hospitality.

We try to know our guests before they arrive. We do research, and at every service meeting the staff discuss the 40 people who will soon come to eat at the restaurant to find out where they come from and why they have chosen to come here. Have they eaten at Noma before? Do they have any preferences or aversions? Is this the meal where he will propose to her?

When the guests come through the door, we welcome them to our home. We embrace them with the form of hospitality that we believe in, and luckily the guests usually recognise this and feel welcome and relaxed. That makes them receptive towards what we offer them. And isn't that precisely what all businesses and organisations try to do?

When you do try to communicate to – and with – your main public, I believe that the best way of doing it is through a "physical meeting". This happens to be a part of our profession, but everyone can do it. It's not just in the restaurant business that you can do it.

Create your own physical meetings and get close to those who mean most to you. The potential reward is apparent; if you do a good job here, it could be that your main public will become your ambassadors/followers and become those who spread the good word about you and your organisation. That's a vital asset that can have great importance for your business.

But of course you must be careful how you do this. Under all circumstances you must respect your counterpart. This is based on trust, and you must never take that for granted.

At Noma we serve only about 80 guests a day, but if you think about it, we host ten parties five times a week and are hosts to eating guests from all over the world, so the echo from creating a unique, personified experience can be more powerful than almost any other type of advertising. In any case it is more lasting. If you've given anyone a meal, they will remember for a long time, they'll tell others that they've been there and tasted it, and they can confirm that it's not just hyped. It's for real.

JOHAN BÜLOW
All fired up

Johan Bülow is an entrepreneur, known for his company Lakrids, and was named Leader of the Year in Denmark in 2014.

As an entrepreneur and leader, Johan Bülow has become synonymous with the word 'lakrids' – Danish for 'liquorice'. That is due to his ability to transform the raw, fibrous liquorice root into exclusive products that consumers over most of the globe have adopted. Bülow's growth venture is called quite simply "Lakrids", and at the time of writing the company is represented in 20 countries and has turnover amounting to a three-digit million figure. Love of liquorice is so deeply ingrained in the young entrepreneur's self-image that on Facebook he is known as Johan Lakrids Bülow.

I believe that if I called Johan a liquorice nerd, he'd take it as a big compliment. But what else characterises this entrepreneurial young man from the Danish island of Bornholm, whose career is storming ahead and who has adorned the front page of a large number of media because of his passion for a root that for some people is a remedy against coughs and stomach aches, but for Johan is the central element in creating a unique and exclusive taste experience?

As the editor of this book I talked to Johan Bülow about thinking as an entrepreneur, authentic leadership and actually a whole lot that wasn't about liquorice …

Although many people may not really consider Bornholm as the stronghold of entrepreneurship, I have seen in many reports that you believe the island's entrepreneur environment has been quite decisive to your success. Can you tell me a little more about that?

As a child I grew up in something you could in many ways call an entrepreneur community. Close to my childhood home were a micro-brewery, a chocolate factory, an ice-creamery, a sweet factory and a glass-blowing workshop. In addition, I grew up with a mother who was one of the most entrepreneurial people I know.

As young as the age of 16 years my mother borrowed money from her father to start a grill bar in Aarhus. Then she threw her interest onto glass-blowing, and right now she is involved in bead production in Ghana. She has always inspired me greatly, and my mother has given me the love of entrepreneurship as a way to live out one's childhood play and dreams.

Bornholm as an entrepreneurial Mecca! Wow! It wasn't limited to the street you grew up in, was it? What about your school, for example – did that also hatch out budding entrepreneurs?

Yes, it did, actually. Now you're going to get some wild facts from Johan's school! Over three years, my little school with about 150 pupils hatched out a liquorice-maker, the restaurant Kadeau (editor's note: named as one of the world's 50 best restaurants), the singer Aura, and the entrepreneur Nicolas Michelson, the man behind the company Airhelp, which has been named by CNN as one of the world's 30 most promising new businesses.

I think that's because when you grow up on Bornholm, you have a very great urge to distinguish yourself afterwards. That is, do well as an islander. In addition, such a small island community means that there arises some odd form of self-regulation when it comes to product quality. By that I mean that if you really make a shitty product, but try to convince the world around you that it's nevertheless fantastic, then the gossip starts on the island, and that's not nice. Therefore, we basically want to do things well as islanders, and in my view this focus on quality is completely essential for one's success as an entrepreneur.

Precisely this thing about quality is also something I've thought a great deal about as an entrepreneur. Sometimes I believe you forget completely about that element when you want to explain why some businesses are successful, while others fail. Why are Apple, Facebook and Skype, for example, successful with their efforts, when there are plenty of similar products and services? Including some that have come both before and after them.

Is that perhaps also to a large extent due to the ability of the companies mentioned to deliver a user interface and a user experience that are superior to those of their competitors in terms of quality?

Yes, I agree completely, and the same thing applies to Lakrids. We ask our customers to pay DKK 70 for 150 grams of liquorice. You can only get people to pay that again and again if they think it's worth the money. The key words for me have been thoroughness, focus, product and passion – plus a lot of hard work, of course.

When you're talking about liquorice, one senses that you are both a nerd and extremely passionate about liquorice. How have you as leader been able to transfer some of that passion to your staff? One of the challenges facing successful entrepreneurs can be that the rest of the team doesn't always share one's enormous dedication and motivation.

I think there are two answers to that question. One of them is that for us, quite fundamentally, you should feel that going to work is cool. You'll never find an employee at Lakrids who goes to work with the thought of taking time off. They won't be here very long. The other answer is that as leader, you must have the ability to invite your employees into the business and let them develop it without you interfering all the time. I always look on new staff appointments as a way of buying competencies that can give Lakrids something new and teach me something. The new recruits give us some competencies that will help strengthen both the product and the entrepreneurial culture at Lakrids.

Entrepreneurial culture – exciting. What do you mean by that in practice?

As in any other growth business, we also have focus on performance. When you perform well, you should be rewarded.

But in addition, all the time I also try to develop a culture that has small elements built in, which give the individual employee an opportunity to take joint ownership and act as an entrepreneur. I can give you a couple of examples: When for instance you turn one of our latest liquorice tins upside down, you'll see "cooked by Morten Fitzner" (or some other name) on the bottom. That's the name of one of the people who helped secure the high quality in the production, and they should be given credit for that in a very visible way. That naturally gives them en enormous feeling of joint ownership and pride.

With regard to our sales and marketing departments, I give the employees responsibility for events where the individual sales or marketing person has sovereign responsibility for arranging a given product event. If they have the idea of involving a Michelin chef, then they'll simply ring that person. They get things the way they want them, and therefore they'll involve themselves in quite a different way than if they just carried out orders.

You've told me that you're just as much an entrepreneur as you are a leader. And still are today. What is a typical day like for Johan Bülow?

Well, that's what I think I am. Even though I do have a large leadership responsibility for my employees, of course, and that's a responsibility I take very seriously, there is still a great deal of entrepreneurship in the job I have. Although I'm the CEO, I have tried to place myself in the organisation so I am a very product-focused CEO. I'm not the man who runs through the figures in the greatest detail and lists our KPIs; instead, I'm the man who runs about all the time and gets involved in everything that's happening in the company.

Our lawyer likes to say that every time he meets me I'm running around all fired up and he can see that in my eyes. SHINING EYES is what he calls it. And being all fired up is something that infects my employees.

In addition, my involvement in the details also means a lot to them. I can remember a few years ago, when the staff on Bornholm suddenly couldn't get a liquorice pot to boil. In that situation I decided to jump on a plane to Bornholm that same morning to help them sort it out. There's no doubt that a CEO who's immediately involved in the details of his company also gave some 'street credit'.

In 2014 you were named Leader of the Year, and I've always regarded you as a very authentic person – and leader. In this book we talk about the authentic leader as one who dares show his feelings, mistakes and weaknesses, for instance. Does that describe you as a leader?

I can't help showing my feelings, because I am so proud of our product. The worst thing for me would be if people ate a piece of our liquorice and then spat it out in a rubbish bin. That would hurt me enormously. In addition, I am very open towards my employees. For example, I've been at a management meeting and told my colleagues that I felt I was under extreme pressure and needed to go home and take care of myself. That occurred during a period when I didn't remember to respect my boundaries, and I could feel in my body and my soul that something was wrong. Luckily, I've learned to find the balance today and that's super important when someone like me is also highly ambitious as a father and husband as well as a leader.

Lastly, Johan … Today, Lakrids as a company is present in 20 countries. What is the dream – for the company and for yourself personally?

I'm convinced that I'll be running just as fast in 20 years' time as I do today. If I wanted to retire, I could have done it three years ago and lived on the money for the rest of my life. But I wake up every morning with the urge to make a difference both for my family and my company. I have this constant wish to do everything a little better than the market and, luckily, that drive is infectious. And, well – we're back at that all-fired-up look in the eyes …

JONATHAN LØW
Editor of Secret no more!

Jonathan Løw is a Danish entrepreneur and co-founder of 4 startups. He has been named one of Denmark's 100 most talented leaders and has won a number of startup awards.

In addition to being an entrepreneur, Jonathan Løw is the former Head of Marketing at the KaosPilots, Investor at Accelerace and Head of Online at Bog & idé. His previous books, Listen Louder and GURUBOGEN, made it to the top of the best seller-lists in 2015 and 2016.

For more info, speaking engagements etc., please check out
www.jonathanloew.dk